In a world full of distractions, this bo a trusted friend to take a deep and wind has been knocked out of you, get your feet reset, and lean back into the strong arms of Jesus.

—Bob Goff, author, *Love Does*, *Everybody Always*, *Dream Big*, *Undistracted*; sweet Maria Goff's husband; Megan's good friend; chief balloon inflator at Love Does

Relaxed is a tender, vulnerable book from a woman surprised by one of life's most painful losses, yet it is not a grief book. Megan Fate Marshman's husband, Randy, died unexpectedly in 2021, and the book is infused with Randy's wisdom, personality, walk with God, love for Megan and their boys, strength, and character, yet it is not about Randy either. This is a book about learning to fully trust God with everything we have and are, and how to relax into all of the moments of the life God gives us.

—Kay Warren, cofounder, Saddleback Church

Megan is the epitome of relaxed, California cool, but it's clearly Christ in her that has brought the kind of peace that transcends the deepest losses. Her transformational words, hard won and true, are an invitation to receive the rest and hope and joy available when we finally let God lead us through life's good/hard dance.

—Katherine Wolf, author, *Treasures in the Dark*, *Suffer Strong*, and *Hope Heals*

In her compelling, open-hearted style, Megan Fate Marshman takes us on a journey toward peace in our anxious age. *Relaxed* is a book that surprises, comforts, challenges, and inspires. It's a life-changing read.

—Dr. Amy Orr-Ewing, author; speaker; theologian; honorary lecturer, Divinity University of Aberdeen

Megan Marshman has a unique ability to cut to the heart of the matter with the most poignant truth, but in a way that feels like salve on burn wounds. Megan shares candidly about her own experience of striving for needlessness and the rest and freedom that come from learning to trust God with all our hearts. We all need this message in this loud, chaotic, independent world.

—DAVE DUMMITT, SENIOR PASTOR, WILLOW
CREEK COMMUNITY CHURCH

If there's something we could all use a bit more of, it's not just rest, it's resting God's way. With *Relaxed*, Megan takes us on a journey that leads us all beside stiller waters, where the restorer of our souls meets us every time.

—PRESTON MORRISON, LEAD PASTOR, PILLAR CHURCH

Finally! In our culture dominated by hurry, busyness, and noise, someone took the time to lead us step-by-step into the freedom of Jesus' easy yoke and light burden, and not just give us more verses about it to put on another coffee mug.

—CHRIS BROWN, LEAD PASTOR, NORTH COAST CHURCH

In a hurried, frantic, do-it-yourself, and count-on-yourself world, this book is a powerful reminder of Jesus' example to slow down, be present, and lead at Jesus' pace.

—BRAD LOMENICK, FORMER PRESIDENT, CATALYST;
AUTHOR, *H3 LEADERSHIP* AND *THE CATALYST LEADER*

Relaxed is a welcomed respite in vexing times. Megan has given all of us an opportunity to engage Jesus' peace as we trust Him to lead us wherever we go.

—BRENT ELDRIDGE, LEAD PASTOR, ARBOR ROAD CHURCH

There are gifted communicators who entertain, educate, inspire, and impress us. There are others whose life and faith help us grow just because of who they are. They influence us. Megan is both. I learn from and am impressed by her gifting, and I'm convicted and challenged by her life. I'm grateful for this book and for the way she models what it says.

—CHAD MOORE, LEAD PASTOR, SUN
VALLEY COMMUNITY CHURCH

In *Relaxed*, my friend Megan teaches us how to relinquish the illusion of control by trusting, connecting with, and surrendering to Jesus. Every single person needs to create margin in their life to read this profound work, which shows the sacred way, the medicine needed for our souls, so that we can experience the confidence and peace that Jesus is willing to provide.

—BRENT CROWE, PHD, VICE PRESIDENT,
STUDENT LEADERSHIP UNIVERSITY

There are few leaders I respect more than Megan. Her choice to live out this Jesus faith, in the midst of extremely difficult circumstances, gives an authority to the words she writes. Rest and relaxing come only from trusting God, and we need that more than ever! I'm so thankful to know Megan and for this incredible work.

—TYLER REAGIN, LEADERSHIP AUTHOR;
SPEAKER; COFOUNDER, THE 10TEN PROJECT

Megan Fate Marshman is one of the most invigorating people I've ever been around—bright, witty, winsome, wise. But her vigor has not come cheaply. Hers is not the thin optimism of the unbereaved. Megan has learned to trust Jesus through terrifying trials. And in her new book, *Relaxed*, she teaches us to do the same. This book is dripping with shalom.

—DANIEL GROTHE, PASTOR; AUTHOR, *THE POWER OF PLACE*

In a world where anxiety, depression, hopelessness, and uncertainty swirl around us like an unrelenting fog in stormy seas, Megan artfully points us back to our one true source of hope and direction: Jesus.

—BRIAN WURZELL, PASTOR OF CREATIVE PROGRAMMING, PASSION CITY CHURCH AND PASSION CONFERENCES

RELAXED

OTHER BOOKS BY
MEGAN FATE MARSHMAN

*Meant for Good: The Adventure of Trusting
God and His Plans for You*

SelfLess: Living Your Part in the Big Story of God

Walking with the One
Who Is Not Worried
about a Thing

RELAXED

Megan Fate Marshman

ZONDERVAN
BOOKS

ZONDERVAN BOOKS

Relaxed
Copyright © 2024 by Megan Fate Marshman

Published in Grand Rapids, Michigan, by Zondervan. Zondervan is a registered trademark of The Zondervan Corporation, L.L.C., a wholly owned subsidiary of HarperCollins Christian Publishing, Inc.

Requests for information should be addressed to customercare@harpercollins.com.

Zondervan titles may be purchased in bulk for educational, business, fundraising, or sales promotional use. For information, please email SpecialMarkets@Zondervan.com.

ISBN 978-0-310-35829-9 (audio)

Library of Congress Cataloging-in-Publication Data

Names: Marshman, Megan Fate, author.
Title: Relaxed : walking with the one who is not worried about a thing / Megan Fate Marshman.
Description: Grand Rapids, Michigan : Zondervan, [2024]
Identifiers: LCCN 2024006703 (print) | LCCN 2024006704 (ebook) | ISBN 9780310358275 (trade paperback) | ISBN 9780310358282 (ebook)
Subjects: LCSH: Rest—Religious aspects—Christianity. | Relaxation—Religious aspects—Christianity. | Leisure—Religious aspects—Christianity. | Stress management—Religious aspects—Christianity. | BISAC: RELIGION / Christian Living / Spiritual Growth | RELIGION / Biblical Studies / Old Testament / Poetry & Wisdom Literature
Classification: LCC BV4597.55 .M58 2024 (print) | LCC BV4597.55 (ebook) | DDC 248.4—dc23/eng/20240429
LC record available at https://lccn.loc.gov/2024006703
LC ebook record available at https://lccn.loc.gov/2024006704

Published in association with The Bindery Agency, www.TheBinderyAgency.com.

Cover design: *Studio Gearbox*
Cover illustration: *Bor Cvetko / Stocksy*
Interior design: *Denise Froehlich*

$PrintCode

For my Randy

"For to me, to live is Christ and to die is gain" (Phil. 1:21).

This book is everything I've learned
since you stepped into the gain.

CONTENTS

CONTENTS

ACKNOWLEDGMENTS

GOD HAS GIVEN me a community of remarkable people to complete this good work that He prepared in advance for me to do.

To my family: Dad, I'm evolving into the person I've always wanted to be—more like you. Mom, your selfless life sets us all up to chase our dreams. Dan and Shirley, my in-laws who embody Randy, your ready availability helps the boys and me thrive. You raised an incredible son and remind me of what he was like every day. Kimi, you've shared in my grief, celebrated every joy, and carried me through every trial. Foster and Jedidiah, being your mom is the highlight of my life.

To my friends: "Deeper with Jesus gals," your friendship has been a grounding force. Thank you for consistently pointing me toward Jesus. Erika Kimura and Haley Tyler, your enthusiasm and willingness to read the earliest drafts while sitting next to me on my couch provided the encouragement I needed to press on. Thank you for opening your hearts to the content. I'm so glad we're friends.

To my writing team: Jeff Carter, thank you for generously lending your God-given, brilliant theological mind for meticulous editing. Josh Harrison, thank you for reviewing the entire manuscript and inspiring me toward deeper thinking and winsome writing. Meredith Hinds, your editing prowess not only refines words but also gives me the courage I need to keep telling stories. My team at the Bindery, thank you for introducing me to the wonderful team at Zondervan and journeying alongside me through each of the production stages. Carolyn McCready, you're a pro.

I offer this last acknowledgment as a prayer:

Heavenly Father, I bow in gratitude to Your Son, Jesus Christ, the ultimate giver and designer of life. Thank You for using all things to form me more into Your likeness by Your Holy Spirit. Thank You for guiding my life to be in You, as You're in me. Amen.

INTRODUCTION

Relaxed

Trust in the LORD with all your heart
and lean not on your own understanding;
in all your ways submit to him,
and he will make your paths straight.

DALLAS WILLARD ONCE had this great response when asked if he could describe Jesus in one word. He sat back, took a deep breath, and responded, "Relaxed."[1]

As we know through Scripture, for Jesus to come across as relaxed doesn't mean He didn't grieve or get angry or feel the weight of the world on His shoulders. But it is clear that He was never in a hurry to be anywhere other than where He was, fully present with whomever was right in front of Him, trusting and obeying His Father's way. Does the word *relaxed* describe you?

It can.

And for those in Christ, it will!

But for many of us, it probably doesn't right now. Often the words we would choose to describe our lives would be something like *distracted* or *hurried* or *anxious*—any word besides

1

relaxed. This is because we have been unconsciously trained to figure out and live the Christian life on our own, and the results are weariness, confusion, and burnout. Why do we succumb to the cultural norms of independence and anxiety instead of living into the relaxed life of Jesus? How will we ever walk with God when we're so preoccupied with figuring it all out, living better, sinning less, and loving more, all while praying without ceasing? It seems impossible, and it is—on our own.

One of the greatest counterfeits to living like Jesus is living in Christian autonomy—trying to be like Him *without* Him. I'd sum up autonomy in this context with one word: self-reliant. The problem, of course, is that, from start to finish, the Bible defines the Christian life as one of dependence. When we fall into autonomy, into relying on ourselves, our lives become burdensome, worrisome, and anxious. We fall for distractions and our faith becomes pretense. We become experts at the routines, the lingo, and the habit of acting Christian while rarely engaging in a real, conversational relationship with God. The one we claim to be following is relaxed, but our lives aren't. We're burdened and bothered and ashamed and grieved and angry. We want to grow, but we fear it's just going to be more ineffective work—work we've put in before that felt like a burden. We perform in prayer (*if* we pray) as we hustle to become better Christians, while experiencing no real power, bearing little to no eternal fruit, unintentionally playing a part in God's story we were never intended to play: the one in control. It's a problem.

Jesus said, "Apart from me you can do nothing" (John 15:5). It's a qualitative statement meaning you can do a lot of things, but they will amount to nothing. But man, we can spend a lot of time and energy worrying about a lot of things, can't we?

I have been an autonomous Christian who doesn't know how to slow down and just *be* with Jesus, and I have tasted the slow, powerful, relaxed life with God that I see in so many of the people whose faith I admire. I've had good conversations with Him and felt at ease even as the chaos around me remained the same, but then I've simply forgotten to prioritize time with Him the very next day. If you're discouraged by this on-again, off-again life with Jesus, don't worry. Remember, the goal is not striving. Striving for something is what got us into this mess in the first place. The goal is proximity, nearness (and awareness of our nearness) to Jesus.

It's all going to be okay.

Really.

It is.

I wish I could look you in the eyes and tell you this.

Stop for a moment. Take a breath. Slow down.

It's going to be okay.

God has already grown you to where you are today. He already knows where you'll be in five years. He's moving in your life right now. This is good news: you, the one who doesn't have to be in charge, can relax. You don't have to figure it all out right now if you're in relationship with the Sovereign One. God's sovereignty means He's in control of everything. Even as we make choices, He masterfully weaves them all together to fulfill His purposes. He knows where you've been. He knows where He wants to take you. He knows how He will get you there. He wants to walk *with* you, so you can relax.

God's plan is not to fix us or our problems or our emotions quickly. His pace toward our long-lasting, endurance-building growth is more of a walk. Nothing about the verb *walk* suggests speed, hurriedness, or even productivity. You put one foot in front of the other and you're taken somewhere else. But when you walk with God, you're taken in the direction He knows is best. But maybe the direction He's taking you is different from the direction you were hoping for. More downward than upward. Deeper rather than wider. More about endurance than speed.

That's where things get challenging. Endurance is hard, and maybe you've gotten tired and given up along the way. The good news is that all you have to do to start walking again is take a step. If you trip or fall, you can get up and start walking again. God has unending grace for you, and that's what His grace is like. It's simple, and it moves you forward. Like a parent watching a toddler learning to walk, God is not angry or surprised when you miss a step. He doesn't shame you for your misses. He lovingly encourages you to get up and take another step. No sprints or marathons are needed today, friend. Just take another simple step, knowing God goes before you (He leads you in His sovereign path), is behind you (He knows where you've come from), and dwells within you (His prayers for you are effective[2]). Walking with God becomes more natural over time.

He greets us warmly with His nonanxious presence, inviting us to just take another step with Him toward Him and forgo autonomous faith. We can do it, one step—or fall—at a time. But don't just take my word for it, listen to His:

> Trust in the LORD with all your heart
>   and lean not on your own
>   understanding;
> in all your ways submit to him,
>   and he will make your paths
>   straight.
>
> —PROVERBS 3:5–6

"He will." Did you catch that? In the end, *God will* make our paths straight. I think some of us would be more comfortable if the verse ended "and you will figure it all out." Scripture has a better promise: He will. He was already working before you picked up this book, and He will work whether or not you finish it. While you can't fix yourself, you do have a role to play. You don't have to have the answers, you just have to be near to the one who does.

TELL HIM

This book is about journeying *with* God, not attempting to do good things on your own without Him. If you finish a chapter and nothing seems to change, tell Him. If you want to pray more, tell Him. If you don't pray more a week after wanting to pray more, tell Him. We can stop letting our good or failed efforts hinder us from relationship with God as we tell Him what we feel and think. Are you disappointed in yourself because you've long forgotten the truth gleaned from a clever sermon or an insightful blog from a month ago? Tell Him. Are you angry with yourself because you can't seem to figure out how to stop being so anxious? Tell Him. Do you feel guilty? Tell Him. That's walking with Him. That's the direction He's taking you. That's His path.

You have no need to worry about the journey, though, friend. Instead I invite you to relax. At the end of each chapter is a "Go to God" moment to help you remember to talk and walk with God about whatever comes up in your life. Stop and close your eyes and be with the one who loves you the most. You can bring the good, the bad, the feelings of being disappointed in yourself because you can't seem to figure out this Christian life, and you can come out of hiding and take one step toward God by sharing it honestly with Him. He has been drawing you toward Himself this whole time.

In the chapters ahead we will journey through Proverbs 3:5–6 and see what happens as we trust His sovereignty more and our autonomy less. As we do, we will uncover the way of peace, the path to joy, and the relaxed life of Christ in us.

1
PART

Trust in the Lord
with All Your Heart

CHAPTER 1

TRUST IN THE LORD

Trust in the Lord with all your heart
and lean not on your own understanding;
in all your ways submit to him,
and he will make your paths straight.

YOU SHOULD PROBABLY know right off the bat that I'm a widow. My husband, Randy Marshman, died of a surprise heart attack and went home to heaven at age thirty-six on February 21, 2021. I know that learning this feels abrupt, alarming, and wild. It still feels that way to me.

Within months of his death, I noticed a tendency in myself: I took pride in not needing anything or anyone. You'd be surprised at what you can do after a few YouTube searches. So far I've fixed cabinets, changed windshield wipers, carried two sleeping boys off an airplane while towing three suitcases, and fixed a sprinkler, all without asking anyone for help. This stubborn independent streak is common among widows. We hate being dependent. Humanity at large has similar tendencies.

In our culture, independence is a virtue, but it's a hindrance in the Christian faith. Being dependent on the Lord is the root of what it means to follow Him, and yet my friends, coworkers, and family—Christian or not—will forever encourage me when I accomplish something unaided. Our cultural norm of "you are better if you can do this by yourself" isn't going anywhere. If we don't understand it, we'll continue being tempted toward autonomy: the tendency to live our lives, even our faith, trusting in ourselves alone. If we continue living autonomously, we'll miss out on some really beautiful parts of faith—things like intimacy with God, contentment, humility, and peace—and, rather, we'll continue the cycle of self-reliance, stress, and anxiety. When you boil it down to its essence, faith is nothing more than dependence. It is acknowledging that God is God and we are not, and that we need Him for absolutely everything. It is relying on God for what we are tempted to rely on ourselves for. The struggle of dependence is not a matter of who is in control, for God is the one truly in control. It's about what kind of relationship we want to have with the one who is in control, a choice between a competing or submitting relationship. A dependent relationship with God goes beyond a mere power dynamic; it delves into the nature of the relationship.

Do we want a relationship where we strive independently, sidelining our awareness of His sovereignty, or are we yearning for a relationship where we engage in heartfelt conversations with God, forsaking the need to figure everything out on our own? Dependence requires our humility—acknowledging our need for help, voicing our worries and hopes, and opening our plans to His guidance. Relinquishing independence, we can humbly welcome and find joy in the gift of a divine relationship in which we don't have to bear the burden of control.

In my life after losing Randy, I have been awakened to a profound awareness of my needs. As someone who has always prided herself on being useful, strong, and independent, it triggered negative feelings when anyone asked, "What do you need?"—feelings of uselessness, weakness, and dependency, all emotions I was incredibly uncomfortable with. Now, years into my journey, I'm discovering the surprising gift of those feelings. When I let them, they lead me to rely on my greatest sources of strength: God and others. On this journey of grief, I am reminded that my very existence is woven with a need for God, hope, purpose, and human connection. Although death may wear the mask of a robber, grief has unexpectedly bestowed on me two remarkable superpowers:

1. I now know I can't do this life alone. Neither can you. Thankfully, neither of us has to.
2. I care a whole lot about the things that really matter and am finally beginning to care a whole lot less about all those things that really don't. In the scope of eternity, worrying about impressing others, owning more or better or bigger or newer stuff, or accumulating more social-media followers is lessening in importance.

IMPOSSIBLE MATH

I remember sharing with my closest group of friends in that first week after Randy's death that I felt like, ten years into marriage, we were really starting to live into the truth of two becoming one, that we were finally on a journey of living into that reality.

Ten years in, I was experiencing Randy's joy with him, holding his greatest sorrows, and he was doing the same for me. We were experiencing the oneness our covenant promised. It was beautiful. Then the unthinkable happened. Turning to the friends who sat with me during that awful week after, I said, "I was finally beginning to understand the crazy math of marriage, two becoming one. But what happens when one loses one?"

My friends are mature enough not to say anything quick or shallow in a moment like that.

"When one loses one, how does that math work? Does it mean I lose myself?"

We all sat in the grief together, hating math, like always.

Nobody had an answer. It would have been the wrong day for an answer anyway. A year later a friend addressed my math. "You know, I think I know a bit more about the math you wondered about in week one."

I knew exactly what she was referring to.

"I've watched you over the past year, and it seems as though half of you is in heaven."

It's true.

On our wedding day, Randy and I were united as one. Our marriage was the journey of learning to live into that oneness. This is true in marriage and true of our faith and trust in God as well. The journey God is taking us on in our relationship with Him is intended to develop our oneness with Him as we rely on His guidance and faithfulness. Now, I realize this all sounds well and good, but how does it work? It means we need to get to know God more—and ourselves. It works the same way it does in marriage. The reason Randy and I increasingly became one over the years was not simply because I got to know him better but also because I got to know myself better. The same is true in our relationship with God.

In his *Institutes of the Christian Religion*, John Calvin asserts both that without knowledge of self, there is no knowledge of God and that without knowledge of God, there is no knowledge of self. True knowledge of God will always open your heart to the truth of its own need and condition. True knowledge of self will always open you to your heart's need for God.

Knowledge of God without knowledge of self leads to theological arrogance, as people measure their growth solely by their knowledge rather than by the humility that understanding both God and self can bring. Perhaps you've heard the adage "Knowledge puffs up" (1 Cor. 8:1). It holds true, unless the knowledge of God and knowledge of self are pursued together. Knowing ourselves and knowing God in tandem can lead to humility.

Pursuing solely the knowledge of God, neglecting Spirit-led self-awareness, can foster arrogance. Pursuing knowledge of self without knowledge of God results in narcissism and self-absorption. This is one manifestation of what Peter Scazzero labels *emotionally unhealthy spirituality*,[3] and it's what we're seeing in the world today. The rugged individualism that has been sold to us for the past fifty years and more has resulted in extreme (institutionalized and celebrated) narcissism, in addition to anxiety. We need both knowledge of God and knowledge of self for transformation. The theological term for this is *double knowledge*: knowledge of God and knowledge of self.

Let me explain it another way. I can know that God is love. I've known it since I was a little girl. But it's not until I grow in understanding my self and selfishness and wretchedness and arrogance and pride and then look at His love for me that I truly see how deep His love goes. His love for me in my badness expands my awareness of the depth of His love. The deeper I go in self-awareness, the more expansive my view of God's love can be. While we cannot understand everything, the more I'm willing to open my heart to God and know myself, the more deeply I can know God.

Another example. I can know that God is sovereign (in control). But it's not until I look at myself and some of my anxieties that I can realize I have an opportunity to know or believe in God's sovereignty more. This may feel backward. What if we view anxiety not as evidence that we don't trust God's sovereignty but as an invitation to grow in understanding how expansive His divine control over all things has always been? The more I become aware of the locations of my anxiousness, the greater awareness I can have of where His power and love can reach. Our anxieties are not proof that we don't trust His sovereignty, they're doorways into intimacy as He reveals the places or categories or relationships where we can know and grow in trusting His care and oversight of our lives more. Our anxieties are doorways, not walls, taking us to intimacy with the Sovereign One, where we can allow Him to help us grow our trust. My anxiety may be the very place God is directing my attention so that I can open that space up and confess, as the dad with the demonized son did in Mark 9:24, "I believe You're the Sovereign God, but as I look at myself, *help!* Help my unbelief!" (paraphrased). Do you hear the double knowledge? I look at God: "I believe You're sovereign." I look at myself: "Help!" It's only as I know myself more that I can know Him more. It's only as I know Him more that I can grow in awareness of what this can mean for myself.

In Mark 9, Jesus adeptly woos the dad of the demonized boy to open his heart to a profound knowledge of himself. Jesus leads the dad to express his worries, asking him, "How long has he been like this?" (v. 21). Of course, we know that Jesus wasn't trying to learn new information; rather, He was extending a relational invitation for the dad to know himself as he shared the depth and duration of his enduring pain. Experiencing pain, worry, and anxiety is not proof that we don't trust God's sovereignty; rather, it can act as a doorway, leading us to the location within our hearts where we can deepen our trust in Him even more as we share it all.

As we begin this journey of trusting God, therefore, we must look at ourselves. This idea of knowing God and knowing ourselves more gives every part of our lives significance. It even gives struggling a purpose. As we cultivate a life of trusting the Lord more, we experience the by-product of a more relaxed existence, recognizing that we no longer need to rely solely on ourselves. Autonomy, or doing it on our own, with its inherent exhaustion, loses its grip, paving the way for a life free from unnecessary worries. But when we do worry, we have an invitation to open it up and explore it with God. *How does He want to meet me where I am right now with expanding awareness of who He is?*

Relax, friends. Wherever you are is right where He's wooing you to relationship.

So we must remain vigilant, examining our hearts with the Holy Spirit to identify areas where we can expand our trust in Him. Realizations about our autonomy, control, sin, anxiety, or fear become a doorway into intimacy, forgiveness, love, affection, and freedom. And the by-product of those? You become less anxious and more relaxed, less guilt ridden and freer.

The first day I believed in Christ, I trusted in Him and not myself for salvation. But it can't stop there. Proverbs 3:5 invites us not to just trust initially but to learn to trust Him more and more, to embark on a journey of embracing and experiencing the already-true reality. I already trust Him *and* I'm on a journey of discovering how to trust Him more. Trusting in the Lord is not a single decision, it's an ongoing relationship. It's an ongoing commitment to choose love and obedience and honesty each day. The initial decision serves as a pivotal starting point, but it is not the whole journey.

I am writing from a unique place in my life, and I don't want to miss the gifts of this season of pain. Grief is the shadow of everything beautiful. Many things in life, even those considered inherently good, like ambition, knowledge, and compassion, can have shadow sides.

Ambition can drive people to achieve great things. However,

excessive ambition may lead to burnout or neglect of other important aspects of life. Knowledge empowers people to grow. It can also be misused or weaponized. Compassion cultivates empathy. But without boundaries, we may burn out or enable harmful behaviors in others.

Even good things have shadow sides.

And seasons of pain come with incredible gifts. Each time I consider Randy and heaven and Jesus, I receive the gift of perspective.

The math of God is abundance: even grief has the potential to expand life and to make love and joy go deeper. But it requires a willingness to open up your life in conversation with God.

Openness is key for all relationships. It's key to letting your heart be loved. It's key to building trusting relationships. I've sat in the grief and allowed it to open me up. I've seen the good and the bad and have found God in both. I've seen my selfishness, my pride, my apathy, and so much more and have found that trusting God doesn't always look like bliss. It looks like honesty, trusting God with the truth of precisely where I'm at, even if I don't like it. Even if I'm mad or sad. Honesty is fertile ground for personal growth because it's the only place we can receive love. This is why so many people have a hard time receiving the love of God. We've become experts in presenting a false self to the world and to God. But it's impossible for a false version of me to receive love genuinely. When we are honest with God, we're demonstrating our trust in Him.

STEP ONE: GO TO GOD

The central theme of chapter 1 is that placing trust in God's sovereignty aligns you with this simple yet profound truth: God is in control, relieving you of the burden of trying to be.

I was standing on my driveway rattling off every care and concern in my life to a trusted friend. She listened intently and compassionately, and in hindsight, I'm realizing she listened patiently. I felt the burden to fix a relationship, to stop being angry, to be more patient with my kids, and to get better at doing my quiet times. Once I finished my list, I was ready for her advice.

She asked, "Do you trust God?"

Her question really annoyed me. "Well, yeah, of course I do," I snapped.

"I thought so. One more: Do you trust God enough not to have to worry about all of it?"

Huh? What? But who is going to worry about all of it if I don't?

My friend wasn't done. Her next question was "Do you trust God's timing?"

"Yes," I replied. I jumped ahead and followed that up with, "I believe His timing is perfect, even if it isn't ideal. It *is* perfect. But that doesn't mean I like it."

We smiled.

She still wasn't done. "Megan, do you trust God's timing for healing it, fixing it, figuring it out, and solving it all, so much so that you don't have worry about it?"

Geez.

She was bringing me back to step one: Go to God directly. The truth was I wanted to be at a later step. I wanted to run ahead and know the entire plan, display the fruit of the Spirit, reconcile the relationship, figure it all out—or at least just get better at prayer right now. What I really needed, instead, was her invitation to consider step one. Had I even said anything to God yet?

I know people who live in step one. I was recently walking down the church hallway, approaching a friend who was days away from the final interview for his dream job. In the two seconds I had before we were close enough to engage in conversation, I thought, *I bet he's nervous. Should I bring it up or just say hey?* I combined both ideas. "Hey! How are you feeling about the big interview?"

He responded, "I feel really good about it."

His tranquility was so shocking that I asked, "How in the world are you so calm?"

He thought for a second and then declared with a smile, "God is sovereign. Even I can't screw it up."

Read that last line again. You're welcome!

My friend knew that if he crushed the interview and got the job, God was sovereign. If he crushed the interview but didn't get the job, God was sovereign. If my friend screwed up the interview and didn't get the job, God was sovereign. If he screwed up the interview and somehow got the job, you guessed it, God was sovereign. He couldn't screw up God's sovereignty and neither can you.[4]

My friend was so connected, walking and talking with God, through the entire interview process that the by-product was a relaxed approach to the big day. The big day was just another day to share what was on his heart and find God's heart toward him. He was loved by the Sovereign One. Even he couldn't screw it up.

The antidote to anxiety and worry and the burdens we carry is confidence in the sovereignty of God. God already knows what's on our minds. If God is in control over all and already knows all, then we have nothing to hide from Him. Our honesty is important so He can meet us where we're at. We try to do more instead of just being with the one in control, but that takes time. The journey God takes us on in trusting His sovereignty begins with a personal awareness of all the ways we don't trust Him. And then being honest about them.

Wait, you might be thinking, *you mean we can talk to Him about the ways we don't trust Him?*

Yes.

It's not like the conversation is going to surprise Him.

However, it might be surprising to us. It was for me. Anxiety is not the ultimate monkey to get off your back. Anxiety isn't even a sin, it's a signal. Anxiety is a light on the dashboard of your soul, signaling to you the very thing you can—and need to—dialogue with God about. The way He often works in my heart is not by taking away the anxiety but by creating a safe place to talk about it together.

The first step in your journey of becoming more relaxed, more like Christ, is to go to Him with everything, even with your anxiety. Not by firmly declaring "I trust You, God" while ignoring your worries. Rather, by speaking to Him about all of the worries and the ways you don't trust Him. Going to God with the truth—even if the truth is that you don't trust Him in an area of your life—*is* trusting Him. Trusting that He is the solution to the problem. Trusting that He will teach you how to trust Him more fully. He grows us and then transforms us as we go to Him.

Dr. Bill Gaultiere, the one who first wrote about how Dallas Willard described Jesus as "relaxed," has given this quite a bit of thought. "Certainly, Jesus has some very un-relaxed emotions in these and other situations. Anguish, excruciating pain, overwhelming pressure, fear, anger, and grief certainly work against feeling relaxed. But the Master shows us that even in crisis or pain a mature person who is attuned to and aligned with God's presence can be calm, joyful, and loving."[5]

Jesus lived a hard life. There were reasons not to relax. But consider this: He wasn't in a hurry to jump-start His ministry. He lived anonymously for thirty years.

During His three years of public ministry, He still made time to go fishing and feast with friends.

When His mom came to him in a hurry, presenting the

problem that the wine had run out at a wedding celebration in Cana, He calmly reminded her that His time had not yet come (John 2:1–4).

He *often* withdrew to lonely places to pray.

When He was caught up in a life-threatening storm, He took a nap (Matt. 8:23–24).

When it was finally time to begin His public ministry, He followed the leading of the Holy Spirit into the desert to pray for forty days.

Becoming like Christ, becoming relaxed, is the by-product of relationship with Him. Love, joy, peace, patience, kindness, goodness, faithfulness, gentleness, and self-control are the by-products of His Spirit in us. The fruit of the Spirit is not the fruit of our effort. It's the fruit, or by-product, of intimacy with our Sovereign God. Becoming more relaxed will happen, not as we try harder to be more relaxed, but as we open our honest hearts to the one who is not worried about a thing.

The most intimate conversations we can have are about the parts of our lives that we haven't figured out yet, when we take the time to process our lives with God. For me, this looks like a conversation with Him where I share what's on my heart. I begin by telling Him the truth about how I feel. It's a conversation where I confess my lack of trust in Him and His timing. A conversation where I confess that I want to get my way more than I want to submit to His.

I DON'T HAVE TO TRUST MYSELF

I've grappled with this thought for years: *I need to trust God more.* Yet time and time again, I find myself relying on my own ability to remember to trust Him. I question how it all truly works and how to genuinely increase my trust in God. Is it as simple as prayerfully declaring my trust? And if so, what comes next? What about when it feels like nothing changes after that declaration—when I say "God, I trust You!" but don't experience any change? No wonder we might give up or succumb to the idea that trusting God is for the spiritually elite. *I'll just keep listening to their sermons and keep trying, or stop trying, and just get pretty good at pretending.*

Is this you? It has been me.

Often when people come across a profound solution to their spiritual problems, a subconscious thought comes: *This is the answer I've been looking for. I will give it a try!* From there they make a conscious decision to change. They think, *I will stop worrying about this issue,* or *I will stop being anxious,* or *I will stop doing this thing and that thing,* or *I will try to pray more when I feel overwhelmed.* However, they make these decisions without going to God at all. We must go to God.

To trust God is not a onetime decision, it's a resolve to open your heart in the relationship continually, to come out of hiding with how you really feel—whether you're disappointed that you're not as far along in your faith as you think you should be, or you don't think you'll ever change, or you're angry with yourself or feeling guilty because this Christian faith / trusting God thing doesn't seem to be working for you. But I don't mean that you should just abstractly "come out of hiding." What I mean is that you should take time to say those things to God, to tell Him (like out loud) what you're feeling, how you're afraid, how you doubt Him and yourself, how you aren't sure you're even going to be able to change. We must take the time to tell those things to God. These thoughts and feelings are in your heart, and God is raising them to the surface. Whatever is felt or experienced in the heart is precisely what can be brought to God (though not necessarily quickly solved by God) and entrusted to Him. That's trusting in the Lord! But it works only if you share with Him. Word by word. Thought by thought. Remember: double knowledge. The more you know yourself, the more you can know Him. Let your knowledge of Him lead you to become more aware of yourself. Then share yourself with Him.

When we're faced with a direction like "Trust in the LORD with all your heart," our hearts must be addressed because our hearts are what God wants to transform—the very stuff and thoughts and emotions that just might be the opposite of all the good behavior we're trying to do without Him. Maybe you're thinking, *God, I don't want to trust You because I'm more comfortable figuring it out for myself,* or *Trusting You feels lazy, like I'm not willing to work,* or *I don't want to trust You because it's really hard for me to trust anyone.* Plenty of people have bought into the notion that "God only helps those who help themselves," which is, of course, diametrically opposed to John 15:5: "Apart from me you can do nothing."

And this, my friends, is why I wrote this book.

I've recently (finally) understood that God wants to do *all* of life with us. He doesn't just save His presence for our eternal salvation and then expect us to grow ourselves by ourselves.

I remember being a junior in high school and assessing how "close to God" I was in relation to how well *I* was doing at my own spiritual disciplines. I was doing so much of the Christian life without Him. I relied on my effort and knowledge over faith and trust. I'd find forgiveness from God in my time of need but then feel the complete weight and burden of a broken relationship with a friend and somehow miss out on doing any part of that relational issue with God.

Trusting God doesn't happen at the moment when we realize it's something good to do; it's available when we think about the fact that we don't want to, when we're lacking a belief that anything will change, or when we wonder whether God hears or cares about our prayers in the first place.

I don't want this book to be a bunch of good ideas that

you'll have to try hard to make work. Or for you to find that they don't work and then pick up the next book for another person's answer.

The goal of this book is for you to go to God with what's in your heart.

Each chapter will be an invitation to relationship with the true God, the one who wants to know you and spend time with you. The one who created you on day six and then took the day off on day seven to spend time with you.

You wouldn't have picked up this book if you didn't have some sort of hope or desire for things to change or for you to do a little bit better at this whole Christian-life thing. So every chapter is meant to get you to go to God in relationship and, in doing so, say yes to His kind invitation to trust in Him with all your heart. You don't have to do a single thing alone.

GO TO GOD

"After" Thoughts

Hey! Megan here. In each of these "Go to God" sections, we're going to put something from the chapter into practice. We're going to go to God instead of just ending a chapter with greater head knowledge.

Don't be worried. Or if you are worried, you can go to God with it. Let's do it together.

Think about something you're trying to work through in your life and say this with me: "I just need to trust God with [blank] right now." Then sit quietly for ten seconds.

Okay, don't quickly move on to the next paragraph. Reread that sentence and pay attention to what you thought about *immediately after* you said that phrase.

Did it go something like this? "I just need to trust God with [blank] right now." *And now I need to do better.* Did you try to motivate yourself with what you need to do next? Did you shame yourself that you're still praying the same prayer? Were you disappointed in God or yourself for your unbelief? Feeling the pressure or burden to figure out how to trust Him with the thing weighing on your heart?

Whatever you thought *after* you said "I just need to trust God with [blank] right now" *is* what is in your heart. If you felt burdened, tell Him. "God, I feel burdened by needing to figure out how to trust You with this." If you felt shame, tell Him. "God, I feel awful that I'm still struggling." If you felt anxious, tell Him. "God, I know You're with me, but I still feel so afraid."

What was your "after" thought?

Now we're talking.

Those thoughts are what we need to bring to the conversation with God. The Holy Spirit is bringing those thoughts out of your subconscious and to the surface. These are incredible opportunities to trust God.

CHAPTER 2

WITH ALL YOUR HEART

*Trust in the LORD **with all your heart**
and lean not on your own understanding;
in all your ways submit to him,
and he will make your paths straight.*

WHEN JESUS WAS asked, "Teacher, which is the greatest commandment in the Law?" He replied, "Love the Lord your God with all your heart and with all your soul and with all your mind. This is the first and greatest commandment. And the second is like it: 'Love your neighbor as yourself'" (Matt. 22:36–39). Love seems to matter most to Jesus. I've always imagined love (or lack thereof) coming from the heart.

I don't know anyone who lived a life of love more passionately than Jesus. Duh, but second place would go to my dear friend Wendy's son, Clayton McDonald.

I went back to school to get my doctorate to learn how to become more like Jesus and to then share that knowledge with other people. Some people don't need to go the long way around, though. I am continually in awe of people like Clayton whose lives already reflect Him so beautifully.

Clayton was diagnosed with leukemia at age seven and underwent two and a half years of chemotherapy, had two-plus years of good health, and then relapsed and underwent a bone marrow transplant. He experienced another two-year period of health, then fell out of remission, underwent a second bone marrow transplant, and enjoyed his senior year of high school before the leukemia returned for a fourth time. At this point it was clear that a cure was not possible. Clayton chose to forgo treatment and live out his final days.

What was he going to do with these final moments?

He used them to reach out to the people he loved. And he didn't pull any punches.

He spoke at his home church, standing in front of his peers and declaring to them with love and compassion: "My doctors tell me I have a few months to live. Don't pity me. I pity you because you think you have forever. I can only imagine you unintentionally wasting your days and your breath consumed with getting people to love you. And you're not crazy for doing it. Don't pity me, though. It's not hard for me to live every day like it's my last because it very well could be."

He then told them about the love of Christ that could satisfy them enough to no longer need to have their hearts filled by anything or anyone else. He welcomed students to respond to the good news of Jesus' love and surrender their hearts to Him, trust Him, and love Him with their hearts, souls, minds, and strength. Dozens came forward.

He then requested a larger audience. They showed up. Same speech. "Don't pity me, I pity you. You're already loved. Let me tell you about it."

I've heard endless stories about this kid and his final few months of life. I've heard about him circling up a group of gals and telling them not to date the high school boys yet because they were not ready. Rather, he said to chase Jesus so that when the boys chased them, the boys would at least be going in the right direction.

I've heard of him going on a mission trip to build a house in Mexico for an underprivileged community. After the mission project, Clayton was late to the bus because, when a street vendor approached him to purchase a cheap hammock, he offered the man double. He asked, "Do you know Jesus?" to which the grateful man responded, "Are you Him?" Instead of heading to the bus, Clayton told the man about a life beyond providing for his family: the man was being provided eternal life by the only one who could satisfy his heart.

I want to be like Clayton, who was a lot like Jesus.

I want to live every day like it could be my last. I want to love God with all my heart. But I don't. Why?

There's a gap between who I want to be, who I hear I ought to be on Sunday mornings, and how I live each day. Why doesn't it feel like I'm growing? Why am I so distracted? Why don't I pray? What is wrong with me? Why don't I live more like Clayton after being inspired by his life?

Why do I hear a good word (from a friend, at church, etc.) and, in that moment, have every intention of acting on it, but then, when the opportunity arises, I don't follow through? Why do I get so annoyed by people? Why do I struggle with the same sin, day in and day out, even though I know it's wrong and genuinely do not want to do it anymore?

Why do I keep trying to fill my heart with anything that seems to satisfy for only a moment? I know God longs to satisfy my heart eternally, but sometimes getting a bunch of likes on social media or a compliment from a friend feels more tangible and satisfying.

Why can't I rest in the truth that God's love is enough?

I didn't realize this was weighing on me so heavily until one of my professors started talking to us about autonomy—that attempt to do the spiritual life on our own. My professor's name was Dr. John Coe, and his lectures about autonomy and spiritual moralism helped me fill in the blanks. Dr. Coe once asked our class this question: "Do you ever feel surprised by what comes out of your life? You know, you do the things you don't want to do, you don't do the things you do want to do, and it catches you off guard?" I sat up a little straighter. No one answered. We weren't sure whether his question was supposed to be rhetorical.

He continued, "The degree to which you're surprised by what comes out of your life is equivalent to your awareness of what is in your heart."[6]

HIDDEN HEARTS

The Bible is clear: our actions come from our hearts.

Proverbs 4:23 says, "Watch over your heart with all diligence, for from it flow the springs of life" (AMP). Of course, we're told to "trust in the LORD *with all your heart*" (Prov. 3:5, emphasis added). And this is why God is so interested in our hearts; they are key to unlocking the lives we were made to live. Salvation in Christ is about more than forgiveness. Jesus wants to lead us not only into forgiveness but also into a new way of being *and* living, and all this will require a significant renovation of the heart. It's about life abundant, which includes spiritual growth, emotional maturity, relational health, physical well-being, and so much more. And these many good gifts He wants to give us start in our hearts.

The problem is, my heart is hidden from me. Yours is hidden from you too.

This explains a lot.

Let's take it back to Genesis 3, back to that first sin.[7] Adam and Eve do the one thing God asked them not to do (sound familiar?): eat the fruit from the Tree of Knowledge of Good and Evil. When God asks them about it, the excuses start rolling in:

- "The woman you put here with me—she gave me some fruit from the tree, and I ate it" (v. 12).
- "The serpent deceived me, and I ate" (v. 13).

With the fall came sin, and with sin, self-deception. After the first man and woman sinned, their eyes were opened, and they realized they were naked. They sewed fig leaves together to cover themselves. When they heard the Lord nearby, they hid from Him. When the Lord called to the man, he said he was afraid because he was naked, so he hid (v. 10). As soon as they sinned, they understood shame and guilt, which led to hiding and covering. It's essential we understand this pattern. We've all become professional hiders and coverers of sin. As sin enters our human hearts, we feel shame and guilt. We're deeply resistant to facing our guilt and shame, so we hide and we cover. No amount of hiding and covering, though, can fix us. Only Jesus can transform our guilt and shame as we stop hiding and covering and, instead, get honest with God. Telling God the truth will open us up to the why behind our behavior, the place where we need transformation.

When Adam and Eve tried to explain their sin to God, they didn't mention their own lack of initiative or lack of trust or plain-old disobedience. Notice, they never lied to God. They knew they had done something wrong and, in a way, admitted as much, but they were totally confused about why they did it. I think they didn't know why they did what they did. Their hearts were hidden from them, and they tried to hide and cover in a variety of ways.

We're no different. While the Holy Spirit of God enters into our hearts at salvation, there is still a difference between the kind of heart that God desires for us and the natural, sinful heart that is still there. While God gives each of us a new heart at salvation (Ezekiel 11 and 36), the flesh (the old tendencies and habits) still remains (Rom. 8:12–13)—and this is where transformation must take place. Salvation doesn't mean perfection. Though, in Christ, we are as loved as we will ever be and our identities are secured because of who He is, we now need to learn to live out those identities, to become who we already are in Christ.

There's a gap, what theologians call the "sanctification gap," between who we are in Christ and who we are on a daily basis. Too often we hear a message at church and agree with the teaching, but we walk away unchanged. We don't realize how the message applies to us personally, and even if we do, we likely don't know how to live it out. Like how do you really put off anger or pray without ceasing? Despite the constant spiritual input, our patterns of sin linger.

Imagine you've signed up for a new gym membership and, on your first day, you get an amazing orientation from a charismatic personal trainer about all the weight you will lose, the muscle you will gain, the abs you will have, and how you're going to feel about yourself. You leave your orientation excited about your new fitness journey. You come back the next day, and the same personal trainer meets you at the door and gives you the exact same orientation. And this goes on indefinitely. Every day, you hear what you're going to (and need to) do but you never learn *how* to do it.

We know we're not supposed to sin, and we really don't want to sin. But we still do—not because we're "not trying hard enough" but because our hearts are hidden from us. We don't know why we do what we do. One way we try to hide and cover (though not intentionally—hidden heart!) is by covering up any part of our lives that doesn't feel right with good behavior. It won't work. We need to get to the roots of the issue.

Quick fixes aren't going to fix our hidden hearts.

We need to appeal to someone who understands what's going on in there.

You know what I'm going to say, right?

We have to go to God.

We need to come out of hiding with God. When God called to Adam and Eve, he sought them out and invited them out of hiding. Even when they refused to come clean, He acted in love toward them. He alone knows our hearts. "He who searches our hearts knows the mind of the Spirit, because the Spirit intercedes for God's people in accordance with the will of God" (Rom. 8:27). God can (and wants to!) change our hearts, heal them, and make them new. He is continuing to pray for our hearts. This is startling! The Son and the Holy Spirit are interceding with the Father on our behalf. God is praying about our hearts! If that isn't both uniquely moving and encouraging, we're not paying attention.

God wants to transform your heart. We tend to use the word *heart* when we're speaking about our emotions, but the Bible doesn't talk about it in those terms. In the Bible, emotions come from our guts (literally our "bowels"), but the heart, in Scripture, refers to the core of our being. Proverbs 27:19 says, "As water reflects the face, so one's life reflects the heart." In Proverbs 23:7–8, we're warned against the begrudging host, "for he is the kind of person who is always thinking about the cost. 'Eat and drink,' he says to you, but his heart is not with you." In Luke 16:15, Jesus says, "You are the ones who justify yourselves in the eyes of others, but God knows your hearts." The heart is what a person really thinks and does—not who she says she is or who he pretends to be. This is why Proverbs 3:5 instructs us to trust in the Lord *with all of our hearts*. We don't trust Him by saying, "God, I trust You." We trust Him by opening our hearts to Him: "God, teach me what's in there."

When we skip over the importance of our hearts—and the reality that they can be hidden from us—we find ourselves mired in spiritual moralism, or the attempt to direct our own spiritual growth. Spiritual moralism is us making an immense effort toward becoming more like Christ without Christ. Spelled out like that, it sounds ridiculous, but I see this all the time. I see it in our culture. I see it in the people I work with and speak with. I see it in our sermons. And I see it in me. This has been my own struggle for decades.

I hear a good sermon on prayer. I decide right then and there that I'm going to get better at my prayer life. So what went wrong in this moment? I skipped a step. I skipped over the truth of what's in my heart and went straight for "trying harder." There's another way to get better at prayer. And, not so surprisingly, it involves prayer. Let's try again. I hear a good sermon on prayer. I decide I want to pray more but wonder why I haven't in the past. I wonder whether I'll get better at it after this moment. And, here's the key, I take those thoughts about prayer to God in prayer. I confess, "God, I want to pray more. Help!" Or maybe I say, "Prayer takes a lot of time. Why don't I dedicate more of my time to it? What don't I believe about prayer? Help!"

The difference between the two ways of trying to grow is significant—and it's a difference that exists in the heart.

GROWING UP

Generally speaking, there are two movements in our spiritual growth:

1. Open our hearts to God.
2. Live differently.

The movement toward God is what empowers us to live differently.

The problem is that, in our attempts to change our lives, we often skip the first movement. We try to change by trying to change. But how is anything going to change if our approach stays the same?

When we're inspired to "do something spiritual," it's natural to skip to the second part—living differently. We try to remember to pray more. We try to remember to read the Bible more. We read more books. We listen to more podcasts. We try to remember to tell people about Christ and what He's doing for us. We have forgotten Jesus' words: "Apart from me you can do nothing" (John 15:5). Instead, we've accepted this American "Christianity" that boasts, "The Lord helps those who help themselves." Again, the difference between dependence and independence.

We struggle with that first movement. Often, our lives change for a moment, but our hearts, the source of our actions, don't change. New habits of the heart form slowly, often much more slowly than we want, but a crash course in trying to change everything we are and everything we do isn't going to work. Instead, we need to dwell in that first movement. Recognize that the one who's going to work the hardest to change your heart isn't *you*. "And we also thank God continually because, when you received the word of God, which you heard from us, you accepted it not as a human word, but as it actually is, the word of God, which is indeed at work in you who believe" (1 Thess. 2:13). He already knows what's in there. Come out and say, "Lord, I need You. I can't do this alone. Teach me what's in my heart."

And then let Him work.

But how can we let Him work? *Let* is an important word because it's passive. It's the type of word used when Scripture talks about *letting* ourselves be filled with the Holy Spirit. Our job is to take our hands off and simply be open to Him. It takes time. It requires vulnerability and time spent with God. By opening to His ways—not our own human work or our feats of spiritual moralism—our hearts can be changed.

Here's an example, just so you can see what "letting God work" and "opening up to Him" look like in real life.

A while ago, my friend Jason was on a walk with his dog, and another dog came and attacked his dog. In the process of separating the dogs, he badly broke his knee. He had surgery to fix it, but the surgery led to extensive blood clots that went undetected for some time. By the time he got to the hospital, he was in a precarious position. The first attempt to remove the clots was unsuccessful, and he was put into the ICU. The following day they tried the procedure again, and it was successful. Because of the trauma and blood loss, when he finally returned home, he was utterly depleted (and anemic).

One morning his wife was wheeling him along in his wheelchair, on that same walk where his dog had been attacked, when three consecutive thoughts formed in his heart and mind. The first was *I don't know.* Yep, he didn't know what the future held, whether he'd be able to walk normally again or lead a normal life.

The second thought was *I can't.* There was nothing he could do to figure things out or make things better; he was helpless.

The first two thoughts were from Jason. The third, which followed immediately on the heels of the first two, was from God: *My grace is sufficient for you* (2 Cor. 12:9).

The first and second thoughts were still true, but because of that third thought, one straight from God's heart to Jason's, Jason didn't need to figure everything out anymore. In a way, we're all in that same position. These two things are, to a certain extent, totally true: we can't know what will happen to us, and we can't control what's going to happen. But what we can do is take it to God, and He can deposit truth in our hearts.

God's grace answered and met and neutralized Jason's utter sense of helplessness. It didn't make those difficult things go away. He still didn't have the knowledge or certainty he wanted, and he was still powerless to fix the situation. But he was deeply and fundamentally okay.

Real change happens when we take it—whatever it is—up with God and then let Him work.

As a young preacher, I remember living in the fantasy that every part of people's lives could change right then and there in the middle of my message and then again in the middle of my next message. On some level, I really thought those messages could change everything. I would try to stir up the willpower of everyone in the audience. I believed students could use their willpower to change their entire lives because I painted a picture of a better life of obedience to God. They would be motivated to change and desire to change, but as I'd later realize, they would soon find themselves disappointed that they didn't seem to be changing.

Martin Luther writes about the bondage of the will in the unbeliever and the weakness of the will for the believer.[8] What we have to do is use our will to remember to go to God and open our hearts. When we desire to make a change, we need to let that willpower take us to God instead of to ourselves. The most important act of the will is to surrender ourselves fully to God. When I am awakened to something wrong within myself, my first thought could be, *Self, you know you can't do this alone. You can't will yourself out of this. It won't work to just work on this harder.* We have to let God transform us. We need to pray, "Holy Spirit, I need You. Look at my mess. God, change me. Give me faith to trust You."

HEALED HEARTS

So why don't we do what we want to do (all the good)? Our habit-uated (made up of habits created over time) flesh is corrupting us. The "flesh" in Scripture is our propensity to sin and live without God. We need to go to God so that we can be healed by Him instead of relying on ourselves to change. If we feel the burden to change ourselves rests solely on us, it makes sense that we'd experience anxiety over our own spiritual growth. We need to stop hiding from God and covering ourselves (in all the ways we try to cover our bad from being seen) and instead be honest with Him, steering away from a life burdened by self-reliance. As Jesus says in Matthew 26:41, "The spirit is willing, but the flesh is weak."

We can be secure in God's love—so secure that we can crack open our hearts and walk around in them with the one who has the power to transform them. When we know we're loved and accepted and forgiven already, we can come out of hiding and search our hearts. We can find a way in us that is not congruent with His life and then open that portion of our hearts to God's love and forgiveness so that we might be changed. Bring it on. Let's open our hearts to God. When I know God will love me no matter what, why wouldn't I want to search my heart and find any unwholesome way within me so that God can lead me in the path everlasting?

We can look at the mess in our hearts knowing there's noth-ing there that is not already forgiven. Nothing will make us less acceptable before God. Now, we may find we're not acceptable to ourselves. Or maybe to others. But let's start at step one. Open ours heart to God. As we do this, we see the truth of ourselves with the one whose love can redeem it all. The love of God now wants to touch every part of our hearts, including our pasts, our patterns of sin, our shame, and our fears.

I want to do the same thing for my children. When one of my sons does something wrong, my job as his mom is to make sure he knows he's loved anyway. I want him to feel so secure in my love that he's willing to go on a journey with me to uncover the why (heart) behind his actions. My greatest desire is that he would feel safe enough to come out of hiding, that I would create an environment without shame. Too often my reaction toward his sin deepens his shame and drives him farther into hiding. I need to let him know that, imperfect as I am, we can deal with it—whatever it is—with Christ. Only Jesus can deal with our shame and guilt. Covering our sin with good behavior can't heal our shame and guilt; only Jesus Christ can cleanse us of both as we open up to Him. As my son's mother, I am radically *for* him. No matter what he's done, I want him to open his heart so that he can grow.

God, our Father, wants nothing less for us.

The simple, profound truth is this: our effort cannot clear us of our shame—only Jesus Christ can do that. We see this interplay in 2 Thessalonians 3:5: "May the Lord direct your hearts into God's love and Christ's perseverance."

It's God's love, not willpower, that is the primary power for change in the Christian heart. It's Christ's perseverance, not our own, that is going to see us through. We are aided not by our efforts to change our behavior but rather by our openness to uncovering the heart (the root) of our behavior to God in honesty. Love of others can inspire us to change, but it's the love of God that can crack open the heart. Our temptation, remember, is to try to change without God, to say in the flesh, "Self, stop worrying." Here's what we can say instead: "God, I'm worried— help me take all of this to You. God, search me. Here's my worry. Let me tell You about it. Teach me about it." Many people want to change by quickly changing behavior because they don't want to look at themselves. But that's not how spiritual growth happens.

Let's recap:

First, we open our hearts and come out of hiding to our God who loves us. Crack open anxiety, worry, envy, jealousy, arrogance, pride, laziness, lust, disobedience. We can't do this in a day because our hearts didn't get that way in a day.

Then we live differently by the Spirit. This can happen through action on our part, but only when we're rooted in God's love for us. Reach out to others in love. Feed the hungry. Read your Bible. Pray even more. As Dr. John Coe said, "Spiritual disciplines don't transform you. They open you to the God who can." Remember who is transforming you. God is the one who can grow you, change your heart, and heal your guilt and shame. You're in good hands—much better hands than your own.

I recently heard about a conversation between my brother-in-law Steve and my nephew Rowan. My brother-in-law was feeling discouraged while working on a significant project, and his ten-year-old son noticed his dad was feeling down and then asked him to sit on the couch so Rowan could play therapist to his dad, who's a psychologist. My nephew loves this game.

"Dad, tell me what's going on."

My brother-in-law settled on the couch, laying his head on the armrest and propping his feet up on a pillow. He sighed, then responded, "Do you have those moments when you feel like the whole team is depending on you and you're afraid you'll let them down?"

Rowan interrupted, "Yeah, actually, this one time—"

Steve interrupted right back with a smile. "Whoa, whoa, whoa. This is about me."

"Sorry, Dad," Rowan said with a smirk. He paused, then grew more serious. And then—you can't make this stuff up—he asked his dad, "How do you think God feels about you right now?"

How we feel about ourselves is not how God feels about us. God wants you to walk on the path of life with, toward, and through Him. You're fully known; you're fully loved. Puritan preacher John Flavel said it well: "Remember that this God in whose hand are all creatures, is your Father, and is much more tender of you than you are, or can be, of yourself."[9]

In your best moments of being gentle with your heart, God is more.

So what do our lives look like when we understand that truth?

Remember Clayton?

He was the teenager with three months to live I told you about at the beginning of the chapter. Clayton made it his mission to tell everyone he could about God's life-changing love for them.

Clayton was terminally ill, but his heart had been healed.

After he gave a few speeches and loved a whole lot of people, his nose started bleeding one afternoon. He knew that this was the end of his life. He called his mom over and asked her, "Mom, can you bring the people I love to the house?"

She started crying and said to him, "Clayton, they wouldn't all fit in the house because you love everybody."

But she had him invite his closest friends until the house was full of people playing video games and eating Panda Express. At one point, Clayton called everyone over to him. He couldn't speak very loudly because breathing was hard, but he told them all, "Guys, I spent so much time trying to get you to like me. Ha. What a waste of time. I don't want to waste time ever again. I want to tell you the reasons I love you." And he did. For hours, he told his friends why he loved them. It was one of the last things he ever did.

Clayton ended his time with his friends that night with a message for them (and for all of us): if you call yourself a Christian and you still have breath, you have work to do.

That work starts with realizing how loved we are. We've

talked a lot about our hidden hearts, but here's the truth: our hearts can be healed when they are brought before the God who gives them everything they need—all the love in the world. Instead of spending your life looking for love, you can love God and everyone else with all your heart just like Clayton did because you can open your heart to the same truth that changed his life: God already loves you.

GO TO GOD

Not Yourself

Do you ever find yourself surprised by your own actions?

I do.

We may be surprised by what leaks out of our hearts, but what leaks out is simply what is in there. When something surprises us (a kid is disobedient, we're cut off on the freeway), we show what's really in our hearts. And if you're anything like me, seeing what's in your heart (anger, impatience, fear) makes you want to change *right now.*

So what do we do? Do we silence those impulses toward change? No, no. But our desire to change should remind us to go to God. Take each of your impulses to change to Him, not yourself.

I need to spend more time with God.

Okay. Step one, go to God. He wants to extend His mercy and forgiveness. From there, He wants to show us why we have trouble with time—why do we spend time on things we know aren't good for us? Why is it hard to turn to God? What's really going on in our hearts?

I really want to stop yelling at my kids.

Instead of "trying harder," take it up with God. Sit quietly with your heavenly Father and ask, "What's my anger about?"

He wants to reveal how our anger that explodes at our kids is really anger at life feeling out of control.

Write down one of the impulses to change that comes up in your heart.

Okay. Step one here is to go to God, not to decide what you need to do better.

What's really going on? What's He telling you? Sit with Him for a moment and write down some thoughts if they come to you.

If we open our hearts, the Holy Spirit, who has been dwelling in our hearts all along, will reveal the truth about us. From this place of truth, God can transform our hearts and, thus, our lives.

2
PART

*And Lean Not on Your
Own Understanding*

CHAPTER 3

LEAN NOT

Trust in the LORD with all your heart
*and **lean not** on your own understanding;*
in all your ways submit to him,
and he will make your paths straight.

AS A CULTURE, we don't like not knowing. Have you noticed? I mean, isn't that why Siri exists? So we can know who won the game, who invented sticky notes, whether the Supreme Court has its own private basketball court with the nickname the "Highest Court in the Land," if it's true that Walmart has a lower acceptance rate than Harvard, or that, in an ironic twist, hippopotomonstroses-quippedaliophobia is the name for a fear of long words. Did you know Cookie Monster has a real name? It's Sid. No, seriously, let me save you a Google search—it's true. You can still search it, though; I know you're obsessed with knowing things.

So am I.

But when we live "just trying to figure it out," you know what we're leaning on? Ourselves. Unless something changes in our hearts, we can't follow the next piece of the proverb: "lean not."

HUMILITY

My husband, Randy, was a humble guy. Last night I was talking with some of his close friends about his unique brilliance. Even though he possessed a variety of skills, he was shockingly humble. I mean, I witnessed him saving someone's life on numerous occasions, and not just at work in the hospital. I'm talking on airplanes. Yet he never bragged about it. Maybe he knew I'd do it for him.

I once asked him how he became humble, and he responded, "I was an arrogant lifeguard." I mean, he must've been arrogant strutting around a pool at sixteen years old wearing only a speedo and a red whistle. He was positioned above people looking down on them. From there he worked hard and eventually landed his dream job working as a firefighter. He was confident—and with reason.

Later, he managed a massive ambulance company and did most of the hiring, firing, and training of hundreds of EMTs, nurses, and medical professionals. Somewhere along the way, he discovered he was training some professionals who had a lot more knowledge about emergencies than he did. While he loved equipping people to help others, he missed helping the hurting people directly. We made the decision for him to go back to school to become a registered nurse.

He said he learned more about the medical field as an emergency room nurse than in all his prior training combined, and that it wasn't until he became an emergency room nurse that he finally knew how little he knew. That's when he became humble in the medical field: when he knew enough to know how little he knew. It's the same in the field of faith.

I was an arrogant sixteen-year-old who thought I knew all the right answers because I grew up in church. Bless my own heart; I had no clue. I knew God forgave me when I confessed gossiping at Bible study but had no suspicion of the power of forgiveness over the secret sins of my heart. I wasn't even aware of the poison of my pride.

Humility is not the absence of pride and sin. It's the by-product of receiving God's love and grace as He deals with the pride and sin that are in us. "Whoever conceals their sins does not prosper, but the one who confesses and renounces them finds mercy" (Prov. 28:13). People who confess develop humility because, in confession, they're going to God with their sin and finding out what He does with it: He gives mercy. He doesn't give you the separation your sin deserves. He knows all of you and loves you completely. Let me emphasize that word *all* one more time. He knows *all* of you and still loves you completely.

That's humbling.

Proverbs 11:2 says, "When pride comes, then comes disgrace, but with the humble is wisdom" (ESV). When you know how much He knows and how little you know in comparison, you're less likely to lean on yourself. It kind of looks like this: a person leaning on their own self hears about a way they need to grow and immediately feels the burden of trying to do the thing that will make growth happen. A person leaning on God goes to God and asks Him to help them remember. They open up their life to Him in prayer, asking Him to reveal why they haven't grown in this area before. Do you see the difference? One person scrambles to change, the other goes to God.

In that moment when you want to change, on whom do you unconsciously lean? If you're realizing as you read this sentence that you've habituated a life leaning on yourself for your own growth, go to God in prayer right now! "God, I want to lean on You and not me. Help!" I imagine that God's delight in our humble approach mirrors how I would respond to one of my little guys honestly wanting to grow and coming to me to ask for help. I'd be so delighted!

Proverbs 3:34 is paraphrased twice in the New Testament, in 1 Peter 5:5 and James 4:6, both of which say, "God opposes the proud but gives grace to the humble" (ESV). What's the way of the proud? Leaning on yourself. What's the way of the humble? Realizing you can't support yourself, you don't know everything, and you can't figure everything out.

Notice how the verse starts: "God opposes the proud." The sentence, like everything, starts with God. Pride is rooted in the belief that the self is God. Pride is self-idolatry. Pride is worshiping yourself, leaning on yourself for understanding, or grace, or righteousness, or anything. Humility doesn't earn us favor with God, but it's the soil in which the seed of faith can grow. Humble people know how little they know.

"Lean not on your own understanding." In other words, don't rely on yourself. If you do rely on yourself and then succeed, it becomes pride. If you rely on yourself and then fail, it becomes guilt or shame. Both arrogance and shame or guilt are manifestations of pride. They are all rooted in insecurity and reliance on ourselves. They just take different paths depending on the success or failure of our self-reliance. When you feel guilt and shame, pride convinces you that you should fix it. And then what happens when you don't? I wonder if this is where you might be right now, seemingly not getting better at the one thing you've been trying to get better at for a while. What do you do then? My suggestion, the best piece of advice I can give you, is to go to God!

Lean On

The word *lean* in this verse gives us an interesting picture. To lean on something is to let something else support you. We don't lean on something we don't trust will hold us up, right? You'll lean on a wall and rely on it because you know it will hold you. You'll sit on a chair only if it looks sturdy. You'll put your full weight on something only if you trust it will hold you. This is going to be a silly image—it's supposed to be—but imagine both standing up and leaning on yourself. Ridiculous, isn't it? This silly picture is the point of what Proverbs is trying to accomplish. The image of leaning on oneself is patently foolish, a logical impossibility. It's like trying to pull yourself up by your own bootstraps. It just doesn't work.

It doesn't mean don't plan. Proverbs 21:31 says, "The horse is made ready for the day of battle, but victory rests with the LORD." You prep, you plan, you think, but you don't lean only on yourself. You have to turn away from self-reliance. I know—this is not easy. It's like when the author of Hebrews tells us to *strive* to enter God's rest (4:11 ESV); we must make every effort not to rely on our effort. This is such an important biblical concept. We can't do the work on our own, but God won't do it without our participation. It's kind of like when Paul tells us in Ephesians 5 to "be filled with the Spirit" (v. 18). We can't fill ourselves, but we have to *be* filled. A passive imperative. It's the idea of what we allow to control us.

So how do we get there?

Get ready, it's backward.

We don't grow ourselves by leaning on ourselves.

The way the Spirit first came into your life, by grace through faith in God, is the same way the Spirit grows your life. The way you were saved is the same way you're sanctified. Sanctification rehearses salvation. You grow the same way you're saved. Growth is less about our efforts and more about believing in His. It's about leaning on Him.

After we receive the unmerited favor of God in the first place by responding to the gospel, the temptation as Christians is to pick up where we think He left off. We come into this new life on His merits but then immediately begin trying to earn our place. We're tempted to rely on ourselves because we think saving us is God's responsibility, while every part of our growth is ours. The issue is that God never "leaves off." Philippians 2:13 reminds us, "It is God who works in you, both to will and to work for his good pleasure" (ESV). Earlier in that same letter, Paul says, "He who began a good work in you will carry it on to completion" (1:6). Notice, He will carry it on to completion, not you.

If you're more patient than you were two years ago, how do you think you got there? More self-control? Where did you find that strength? If you've experienced more joy, what made you that way? Anyone with even an ounce of self-awareness knows we participate in the progress, but God makes things grow.

If I'm honest, I've given myself credit for my personal growth in the past. I've leaned on myself to grow myself. I've felt proud when I feel close to God and disappointed in myself when He feels distant. When did my faith begin to be in myself? I don't know.

Good behavior done in our own strength is the counterfeit to faith. It's not evil, it's just not faith. Good behavior is the appropriate response to a loving God's gracious acceptance, forgiveness, and love, but too often it becomes a means of covering and hiding what's really going on. Good behavior is a wonderful by-product of grace, not a substitute for it.

Let me explain.

What do you think of the word *moralism?* Moralism sounds like something good, right? Well, it's not what God intended as the goal. See, I told you this chapter might feel a bit backward. Stay with me. These truths absolutely transformed my life.

Committed Christians exhibit a genuine longing for personal growth and a heartfelt desire to be vessels for God's purpose. However, amid this devotion, they often grapple with a hidden weight of guilt and shame. Shame and guilt are distinct. Shame is that uneasiness you feel at the core of your being about who you are, relating to your very existence. Unlike guilt, which is about feeling bad for what you have done, shame involves harboring aversion toward aspects of who you are. It goes beyond self-condemnation for actions you've committed and extends to a dislike of facets that comprise your being. While guilt is hating what you did, shame is hating parts of who you are.

Most of us are wrestling with some version of shame. We feel as though we fall short of the maturity we ought to possess. We don't pray or read our Bibles as often as we think we ought to. Thoughts of inadequacy emerge, recognizing that our commitment to these disciplines may not align with our aspirations. A sense of longing prevails as we yearn for the abundant life and spiritual vitality that Jesus spoke of, and we question inwardly why we seem to struggle in that journey of growth. This can leave us grappling with uncertainty as we look around during church, wondering why we don't seem to get it like everyone else. Or, maybe, we're doing all the things for Christ but wondering why we're not experiencing that abundant life Jesus talked about.

When we find ourselves in this place, there are three great temptations: (1) "to despair, tune out," and just accept a dry spirituality, (2) "to act out immorally," since we obviously just can't do it, or (3) and here's the surprise, the "Moral Temptation: the attempt of the hidden heart (not conscious) to try to perfect oneself in the power of the self,"[10] as explained by Dr. John Coe and others. This third place, the moral temptation, leads mature Christians to attempt to use service, ministry, obedience, spiritual formation, spiritual disciplines, spiritual experiences—being good—to relieve the burden of spiritual failure or lack of love and the guilt and shame that result. In essence, in that third place, even mature Christians find themselves trying to relieve the burden that Christ alone can relieve. Don't miss this:

Only Jesus Christ can remove shame and guilt.

Read that last line again. You're welcome.

No amount of effort can ever relieve you of the burden of shame and guilt. Only Jesus does that. Underlying our sinful behavior is insecurity, which flows out of our lack of confidence in the goodness of God and the goodness of ourselves as created in the image of God. Until we address the insecurity, we'll never be free of shame. And the only way to address the insecurity is to trust in the goodness of God.

You cannot remove the shame you feel by your efforts to do good. One more time? You can't remove feelings of shame. You can hide them, cover them, and try to do good to overshadow them. The shame will still remain, typically hidden. It doesn't go away even if your efforts make you feel good for a moment. I'll borrow the words of Dr. Coe to explain why: "The Christian life is not fundamentally about being moral in itself or being a 'good boy or girl.' It is not fundamentally about obedience to a set of principles, it is not most deeply about character or about imitation of Christ as a model external to my soul"[11] (in other words WWJD).

In many seasons of my life, I equated the health of my spiritual life with how good I was at my spiritual disciplines: praying every morning, reading my Bible throughout the day, going to church, discipling newer believers, serving others.

If I did spiritual disciplines faithfully, then God and I felt close (even if I didn't actually feel a thing). If I didn't do them, my Christian life was not going well. As Dr. Coe reminds us, "Spiritual disciplines do not transform you. They open you to the God who can," providing an opportunity for the Holy Spirit to transform you. Spiritual disciplines are a conduit. There are ways in which we participate in the grace of God, but transformation is still a matter of grace, not our work. I had a wrong view of what the Christian life was for far too long. It's not fundamentally about spiritual disciplines, about ministry, about passion—it's about leaning on God.

Let's remember together that catchy Christian cliché: "Christianity is not a religion, it's a relationship." It's not doing, it's being in a relationship with the living God. Christianity is that. It's a relationship. It's not knowledge. It's not understanding. It's not a religion. It's a relationship.

Christianity is not knowing God or leaning on your own understanding of God or your own efforts toward God. The Christian life is God in you taking over.

The Christian life and spiritual formation (becoming like Christ by the power of the Holy Spirit) denounce the moralistic life as a way to find happiness and please God. Doing good is not a terrible place to start, but we must grow up. The Christian life is about Christ, first about what He has done and *then* about our life "in Him." From there, our primary task becomes opening our lives to Him and participating with His life in us. My Christian life is Christ's life in me. It's allowing God to work through me. It's leaning into the one who fully leaned His life into me—resting in Him, abiding in Him, enduring with Him.

So how do we ensure our opening of ourselves to God doesn't become another act of moralism?

Good question.

We can't.

That's why humility is a virtue. *Oh Lord, how we need You.* No wonder Jesus invites us to come, those of us who are heavy laden. We can come to Him carrying our heavy burden of life and confusion and moralism and goodness or badness or anxiety or whatever feels heavy. We can come to Him bringing ourselves and whatever we're carrying.

The life of moralism *is* what we are saved from: a life of trying to be good and pleasing to God in the power of the self as a way to deal with our guilt and shame.

TRANSFORMATION

Let's review.

So being moral is bad? Nope.

Morality (or being good) is the common human solution to avoid dealing with the problem of sin and guilt before God. Adam and Eve did this. Their response to sin was to hide and cover.

I hide and cover too. In response to my own shame, I feel the burden to try to become more moral. Moralism is not doing something bad, of course, but in this context it's trying to do something good because there's a hidden, deep belief that no one can handle my bad but me. The way I, Megan, try to handle all my bad (selfishness, gossip, sinful anger, envy, pride, jealousy) is to lean on myself, just be good (or better), and cover the bad. I think to myself, *I just need to stop getting so angry.* I, like many of us, learned this in childhood. We somehow learned that our parents loved us more when we were being good than when we were being bad. We were told to go to our rooms to figure it all out by ourselves until we could be good again.

And here we discover, again, the beauty of the gospel.

God loves us in the bad.

"While we were still sinners, Christ died for us" (Rom. 5:8). This is what distinguishes Jesus Christ from every other god. This is why the Christian faith is not like every other religion. There is no other God like this who not only tolerates sinners but also runs toward them. I don't know where we got the notion that "God can't look on sin." Jesus is God, and He not only looked on sin all the time but also pursued sinners and hung out with them so much that He scandalized the good, "moral" people.

The world is full of evil, yet God is intimately involved in every aspect of our world and every aspect of our lives. His holiness does not compel Him to look away. In Jeremiah 16:17, God declares, "My eyes are on all their ways; they are not hidden from My face, nor is their wrongdoing concealed from My eyes" (NASB).

The moralist doesn't want anyone to see their failure; they would rather keep working on it on their own.

Yep, this was me, day in and day out, for *years*.

But since I started going to God with the contents of my heart, I've changed. I can look at my failure. I can open up my mistakes. I don't have to keep running to be a better little girl. I can come out of hiding and pray, "God, I need You. I messed up. And I want to know Your love right now. I don't deserve it. Your grace is sufficient, indeed."

I ache for my little boys to grasp this deep, intimate love God has for them. I want their lives to be more than a performance or a cover-up, trying to impress a God who already sees every bit of them.

While sending them to their room to cool off after they make bad choices can be important, I've grown increasingly passionate about using these moments to strengthen our relationship rather than convincing them that their poor choices push us apart. Instead of isolating them to figure it out on their own, I'm now aiming for them to find a safe place *with* me when they make mistakes, a place where the reasons behind their behavior can be uncovered as they're pursued in love. Isn't this the gospel? When we could never be good enough for God, the All-Good One comes to us! We don't cover our bad with our own good, God cleanses our bad because He is good.

My boys must know that their bad choices do not separate them from my love or God's love. Once they know this love, they can steer clear of the temptation to hide behind any type of facade of good behavior that merely skims the surface of their hearts (the source of all their actions). I don't want my kids to learn to perform to earn love; I want them to expose their hearts and then be transformed *by* love.

Anyone trapped in moralism can't know the freedom of entering into their failure or shame or anxiety or pride. The moralist's response to our sin and shame and hiding is to work harder at it on their own. They believe sin management is the most important job.

I'm here to tell you—it isn't.

Salvation, receiving Christ's gracious gift of eternal life, and sanctification, the way salvation plays out in our daily lives as we become more like Christ, defy religious clichés. We're not on a spiritual treadmill. We're members of a transformed community who joined in the dance with amazing grace and continue to participate in it. Here's the thing: we grow by grace just as we were saved by it. Imagine salvation and sanctification not as stiff doctrines but as the means of becoming who you were created to be. Let me compassionately remind you of how this is all accomplished. Salvation has three tenses: past, present, and future. Past tense is justification. The present tense is sanctification. And the future tense is glorification. You've heard the phrase so often you may have forgotten how amazing it is. We change "by grace through faith" (Eph. 2:8 CSB). Grace is God's unmerited favor, and faith is our belief and trust in God. Having faith in God relieves us from having to solely rely on ourselves, a burden too heavy for us. Rather, we come to Him humbly, and God meets us with love and power and forgiveness and grace. As this happens throughout our lives, we become more like Him.

We are saved by God's love, and we grow by it too. We become more forgiving as we receive His forgiveness. And as we find Him in every situation and circumstance of our lives, we can relax. We don't have to hide anything because nothing is hidden from His view. And knowing us, He loves us. Our awareness of His love will transform our lives as we come to grips with the fact that His love has never been dependent on our good behavior. That's awe-inspiring and humbling. Now we're getting wiser.

We can let our sin and anxiety and everything we experience in life take us deeper into relationship with God and awareness of ourselves. As we go deeper, the cross goes deeper, and our dependence on the Holy Spirit becomes greater, too, as we "lean not on our own understanding." We don't have to try to do God's work. We can't use our sin management to grow ourselves into the image of Christ, but by the Spirit, God can!

For a season, I worked for a church curriculum company that provided curriculum for kids' ministry. We wanted to teach kids how to open to the Holy Spirit instead of just learning information and leaning on what they learned to modify their behavior by themselves. While it wouldn't be awful, of course, to have obedient kids, we prioritized creating an environment where kids could flex their faith muscles and lean on the Holy Spirit instead of themselves. We didn't want to create disobedient kids, but we also didn't want to teach them to hide and cover.

We noticed a lot of children's curricula focused on moralism. Too often we were taught to read the story of David and Goliath and think the goal in response was to be more like David.

No!

While David was brave, our goal is not to become more like David, especially if you keep reading his story: he has sex with another man's wife, covers it up, murders the husband, and, well, yeah. Don't be more like David. Do see David's heart and the number of psalms he wrote seeking God's heart as he opened up his heart honestly. In the words of those psalms, you'll find where David leaned in every season of his life.

Oh Lord, how we need You.

I'm thankful we have more of David's story than just his goodness—we have his sin written out and his prayers too. We have an example of someone who learned to stop hiding from God and rather opened up his awful, good, sad, mad, guilty, and exhausted self to God relationally.

Let's recap: spiritual formation's first move is to go to God.

When you hear the next sermon on praying more or living better or sinning less, go to God instead of working harder without Him. See the (very important) distinction?

Remember:

- Moralism leans on you.
- Transformation leans on God.

So where are you leaning?

GO TO GOD

Growing Strong

Where have you been leaning lately?

Invite the Holy Spirit to bring to mind at least two ways you've grown in the past year and write them down here.

1.

2.

Ask God to help as you think through your growth. Did you experience moralism during this time—were you in charge? What about transformation? Name how God was in charge instead.

Let the next few prompts lead you to lean on God and not on yourself as you move forward.

First, sit comfortably.

Close your eyes. Take a few deep breaths. Focus on your breath.

Then focus on God.

Pay attention to the one who is not worried about a thing. If your mind starts to wander, go with it. Don't lean on yourself to draw you back to merely focusing on God when He may be leading you to bring whatever is on your heart to Him.

Express gratitude to God for leaning toward you as you lean on Him regarding whatever is on your heart.

Have you believed you're fully responsible for growing yourself? Open up your answer to God in prayer. (If you'd like, write your prayer in the following space.)

What is on your heart right now as you wrap up this time (relationship conflict, busy schedule, feeling distracted, anxiety)? Imagine yourself opening up your heart to God in prayer and allowing Him to guide you.

End your time with God with a final deep breath. Open your eyes and express thanks for this moment with Him. Thank Him for the growth that's already happening in your life.

CHAPTER 4

ON YOUR OWN
UNDERSTANDING

Trust in the LORD with all your heart
and lean not on your own understanding;
in all your ways submit to him,
and he will make your paths straight.

MY HUSBAND, RANDY, was an emergency room (ER) nurse.

The ER is a messy place. Sometimes the processes, sometimes the people, always the situations and problems. Randy
witnessed all sorts of messes in that place: broken bones, weird
rashes, family dysfunction, the effects of self-neglect, strokes,
accidents, the aftermath of bad choices, and many other tragic
reasons behind an ER visit. I mean, you name it, he probably
saw it. It was a mess, but at least the people were in the right
place.

In recent years, Randy noticed a decline in people's mental
health. One time he shared with me his first response to overwhelmed, anxious patients.

He said he'd stare directly into their eyes. When he had their full attention, he would calmly yet urgently say, "Hi! My name is Randy Marshman. I'm a staff nurse at this ER. There are a lot of things you can do and a lot of things you can't. Here's one thing you *can* do: listen to my voice! Why? Because I'm *really* good at my job."

My husband was typically more of a reserved, behind-the-scenes, I-don't-need-attention-for-my-birthday type of guy, so learning that he demanded attention by declaring his competence felt surprising. I remember asking him, "You'd actually say that? That you're good at your job?"

"Of course." He gave me the same stern look he would give to his patients. I realized I was getting to witness firsthand his trust-building tone as he went on. "Then I'd tell them, 'Listen to my voice,' and say it again. 'I'm *really* good at my job.'"

I smiled as the explanation continued. He was getting people to focus on something other than understanding. There was a lot going on that they couldn't understand: the unknowns of their future, the regrets they couldn't get over, the trials they were facing, the fear and drama of broken people, the sin within themselves, everything. They needed external confidence from someone who understood something about what was happening.

Randy gave them what they needed. He gave them confidence that someone understood and made up for their lack of understanding. He guided their attention away from what they didn't understand and directed them toward someone who did. He didn't give them greater understanding; he just gave them someone to trust. He gave them his words, his voice, his commands, and his steps for getting somewhere helpful. His voice directed them to the things they could control, subconsciously getting them not to focus on the rest of life. He'd get them to breathe slowly. He'd ask simple questions they already knew the answers to, like "What is your birthday?" or "What is your name?" or "Who did you vote for?" At least they'd smile.

Within ninety seconds, their heart rate slowed, their body relaxed, and they released their need to figure everything out—at least for the next few minutes. Did they suddenly understand all the details of what was happening to them? I don't think so. I don't think they would have been able to relax if they did.

So much of the time, I think I want understanding. I go so far as to demand knowledge from God. "God, why? Why did it have to happen like this?" But when I think about it clearly, I realize that I don't want to understand. I want something better than understanding. I want to be able to relax. I want peace. I want God's peace. God's peace is not just bigger than our understanding. Having God's peace is *better* than understanding. And God gives us His peace the same way Randy gave it to his patients, by giving us someone to trust.

HIS VOICE

In the ER, Randy was doing what Solomon did in Proverbs with all his wisdom literature. Randy could've told anxious people to stop thinking about anxious things, but it wouldn't have worked. He gave them a necessary first step: focus on someone who knows something and *listen* to that voice.

Solomon didn't just write down a bunch of good things to do—he pointed us toward the voice we need to hear more than his. The first step is significant, otherwise the book of Proverbs would just be a bunch of wise sayings that we should try to live out by trying harder. This is a differentiator between the wisdom literature in the Bible and other Near Eastern wisdom literature of that time. The Bible alone makes the claim that wisdom is not inherent to humanity but comes through relationship with God.

Solomon isn't saying, "Just follow these rules!" He's assuring us we can't live a wise life apart from God. We can be smart, we can make good choices, but if we really want to be wise, we must start with God.

Solomon starts the book of Proverbs by turning the attention of the people to God, who is the beginning of knowledge, wisdom, and instruction. He directs us to the one who has been in control of everything from the beginning, and he teaches the people how to live (which is, of course, what wisdom means) by coming humble and hungry to learn God's ways.

Proverbs 1:7 says, "The fear of the LORD is the beginning of knowledge, but fools despise wisdom and instruction."

Solomon adds in Proverbs 9:10: "The fear of the LORD is the beginning of wisdom, and knowledge of the Holy One is understanding." Did Solomon say knowing every detail about what's going to happen next is the same as understanding?

Nope.

Not what he said.

Solomon defines understanding as "knowledge of the Holy One." Wisdom is not informational but relational.

And the good news for us is that God is really good at His job. He doesn't need us to "figure it all out" because He already has. He has wisdom for everything, and that's why we have Proverbs. But even as we listen in on what we ought to do to live a wise life, we have to go to God first. We don't read Proverbs for information (the trap a lot of Christians fall into, making it another self-help book) but for relationship, to grow in knowing God.

Much of the time we live in the midst of the unknowable. As a species, our reaction to this reality is pretty negative. Anxiety stats are alarming, and Jesus followers are not immune. I likely don't need to convince you; you've probably already seen it firsthand, in your own life or in the life of someone close to you. So what do we do? We remember the first step is to go to God!

Have you noticed each chapter is telling you the same thing? Go to God, don't go to yourself. Go to God, don't go to your understanding. Go to God, not moralism. Go to God, not another podcast about Him. God is our guide, and He knows the plans. He's guiding you through His Holy Spirit. Kinda like GPS.

In her Bible study book *Discerning the Voice of God*, Priscilla Shirer describes how a GPS works: you enter your destination and obey its instructions step-by-step to get to where you want to go. She likens the GPS to our Guide, the Holy Spirit, who operates in much the same way.[12] If you want to arrive at God's destination for you, then you must be willing to obey the Holy Spirit's step-by-step instructions. God doesn't give all the instructions at once. He gives them one step at a time. Can you imagine that British lady on your GPS giving you all the directions at once? Imagine starting your car, pressing the button, and hearing the following before you even put your car in drive:

"To get to the retreat you drive east out of the parking lot, turn right on North Bellflower Boulevard, make a right onto East Spring Street to get onto I-405 North. It will turn into I-5 North eventually, and then you'll be on that until you get onto Route 99 North all the way to Route 198 South and then take the first exit onto North Plaza Drive. Then you'll make a left and take it all the way down to East American Avenue. Turn Right. Then a left at Cove Road. Don't miss Cove Road. Then turn right onto Route 180 and take it down to the fork in the road where you'll go left. Then you'll be on that for about thirty minutes until you turn right after the Princess Cove sign. It's easy to miss the Hume Lake sign, so pay attention. Then after fourteen switchbacks (after the campground sign, of course) you'll pull right into your retreat location for the weekend. Good luck!"

I hope you had a pencil and paper out to get all that down.

GPS doesn't work that way, and neither does the Holy Spirit. He gives you one step at a time, expecting you to look back to Him for what's next and then to do that over and over again. He even graciously knows how to reroute you and use all your missed turns to get you to where He is taking you. A lot of us want God's will for our lives in twenty years, or five years, or one year, or even five hours from now, but the Holy Spirit is a good guide, not a busted GPS. You're going to get one step at a time because He knows what you can handle. Look to Him. Listen for the next step.

A DOOR, NOT A WALL

In the age of information, we find ourselves swimming in a sea of knowledge, a double-edged sword that promises empowerment but frequently leaves us feeling overwhelmed and anxious. With endless facts at our fingertips, we navigate a world that demands constant decision-making, all while grappling with a fear of the unknowable future haunted by a triggering past.

Solomon, in Proverbs 3:5, imparts timeless wisdom to guide us toward a more relaxed way of living. We find that anxiety loses its grip when we embrace Solomon's wisdom to "lean *not* on [our] own understanding." Let me explain.

Paul writes in Philippians 4:6 (the most highlighted Bible passage on Kindles, by the way), "Do not be anxious about anything, but in every situation, by prayer and petition, with thanksgiving, present your requests to God." Put simply: Don't be anxious; go to God!

Go to Him.

Let anxiety have a purpose: let it lead you to God! Utilize your anxiety as a vehicle to drive you to God.

The interesting thing about anxiety is that it has the potential to do something meaningful. Wild, right? That's probably what James had in mind when he wrote about trials being productive in our lives (1:2–4). Stick with me.

Have you ever tried to get rid of the anxiety by praying about it? I've certainly tried to pray away anxiety. Why wouldn't we? I mean, God might just take it away, and doesn't 1 Peter recommend casting (imagine anxiety on your fishing line) all our cares on Him? But I wonder if anxiety is more like a door than a wall in our relationship with God. Or maybe it's more like a warning light on the dashboard of our lives, notifying us of something that needs to be checked out. Anxiety is our response to something being off. Once we realize it—

Wait! We're going to pause right here with "Once we realize it" and bring to consciousness something that is likely unconscious. How do you realize it? When you're in an anxious moment, it's hard to realize anything, isn't it?

Anxiety can be the very thing that cripples us and forces us to try to lean on our own understanding of whatever we're anxious about. But God also has purpose in it. I wonder whether our problem is less *about* anxiety and more about what we do with it. Let's consider anxiety as a doorway into intimacy with the Father. That is Paul's suggestion in Philippians 4:6.

I'm not telling you to try harder not to be anxious. I'm not going to try to explain away your anxiety or pretend that going to God will just take away the anxiety in the moment. There are other books for that. This book is about not doing anything on your own. This book is about the incredible potential of bringing everything out of hiding and giving it to the Lord, who already knows it all. He knows what we're worried about, and He's not worried about it. He wants you to talk to Him about it, but you don't need to be anxious about your anxiety. You can relax.

It's like the moment you experience turbulence on an airplane. If you rely on your understanding about planes and turbulence (which I'm assuming is very little), your stomach will drop. You'll imagine the worst, clutch the seat for safety, and panic. Everything will feel out of control until you hear that voice from the cockpit. The pilot saw it coming, understands it, and will tell you everything you need to know about it. Pay attention to the pilot's tone and words. When they invite you to buckle your safety belt in a calm, cool, and collected manner, you feel better about it, right? You can trust their words because of their knowledge. Their tone and words regarding the turbulence can give you greater understanding of what your tone ought to be too. (Now, if they're freaking out on the intercom, feel free to freak out as well.)

For those of you living anxiously, let me tell you: this book will be a journey with God. If you lean on someone who is outside of time, you have the potential to hear His tone over the intercom: "Buckle your safety belt. We're going through turbulence, but I saw it coming and I'm in control. I'm taking you to My own planned destination."

Rather than praying for God to just take away your anxiety, open it up with Him, the one who understands, the one who knows the future anyway. Now, realize this: He may not tell you the future, but I can already tell you the tone He's going to use. He's not worried about a thing.

Go to God.

His Understanding

That's what prayer is, isn't it? It's going to God. Prayer even begins with His name: "God." That's why prayer is so powerful from the start: it's going to God and, in doing so, simultaneously not going to yourself. Romans 8:15 says that it's by the Spirit we cry out, "Abba, Father." Only by the Spirit's movement in your life can you even go to Him in the first place. In fact, it's not just that you approach God only by the Spirit, it's that you remember to approach God only by the Spirit. You know what to say only by the Spirit. The only way we know anything about prayer at all is through the Holy Spirit. That's one of the primary things He does in our lives. He teaches us how to pray. God's at work in your life in the moment you pray, "God!" Try it now.

What comes to your mind next?

This, by the way, is how I begin each morning.

In adapting Romans 12:1, I offer myself to God, and it sounds like this: "Heavenly Father, I present myself to You." Then I wait and let my mind wander. It goes all over the place, and then eventually (usually within thirty seconds or so) it goes to whatever has my heart, the thing my mind wants to work out to try to understand. I used to think a wandering mind was a distraction from prayer, so when my mind would wander, I would pause my well-intended prayer to shame myself back to some sort of performance prayer. The problem was I didn't know that a wandering mind is a gift.[13] It brings my mind to the topics that already have my heart, the very things God is interested in talking to me about because they are most interesting to me. He may not give me understanding in any of the topics (He might, I don't ever want to limit God), but in honest prayer, I can be known and receive love from the one who loves me the most. I learned this in class from Dr. John Coe and Dr. Kyle Strobel, who also discuss it in their book, *Where Prayer Becomes Real*:

- "Prayer is not a place to be good, it is a place to be honest.
- "Prayer is not a place to perform, it is a place to be present.
- "Prayer is not a place to be right, it is a place to be known.

- "Prayer is not a place to prove your worth, it is a place to receive worth and offer yourself in truth."[14]

My wandering mind helped my lifeless prayer life die. It teaches me where my heart truly is and what my treasures really are.

So what happens when we go to God honestly, stop performing, and allow ourselves to be known? We spend time with the one who understands us the most. Don't lean on your own understanding. As Proverbs 11:2 states, "When pride comes, then comes disgrace, but with the humble is wisdom" (ESV). Wisdom is living in light of the fact that you can't know everything but you're doing life with the one who does.

Wisdom is not understanding everything—it's knowing how to live well when you don't. It's knowing who to talk to when you can't understand.

GO TO GOD

Eyes on Jesus

The ideas in this chapter make me think of the lyrics to the well-known hymn "Turn Your Eyes upon Jesus." It was written by Helen Howarth Lemmel in 1922. The hymn is based on Hebrews 12:1–2, which states, "And let us run with perseverance the race marked out for us, fixing our eyes on Jesus, the pioneer and perfecter of faith." The song encourages us to go to God, focus our attention on Jesus Christ, and find peace by turning our gaze away from our problems and turning our eyes upon Jesus. By seeking to understand *Him* instead of trying to understand our circumstances, we remember His promises and surrender our burdens and exchange them for God's divine grace and love. Everlasting peace comes from dwelling in His presence.

Turn your eyes upon Jesus,
Look full in His wonderful face,
And the things of earth will grow
    strangely dim,
In the light of His glory and grace.[15]

Remembering that God can handle what's on your heart, whatever it is, take a moment to write a response to the chorus of this hymn.

He may not guide you into a deeper understanding of what's happening around you, but you'll be hanging out with the one who understands. In His presence, you can find your rest. You can relax.

CHAPTER 5

WHERE CAN WE LEAN?

Trust in the LORD with all your heart
*and **lean not on your own understanding;***
in all your ways submit to him,
and he will make your paths straight.

ONE DAY WE will all stand before God.

I've heard this my whole life, but I think about it differently now because my husband, Randy, stood before Him. The moment he died, the "stand before God" concept became very personal to me. My theology and my life collided in a way I had never realized was possible.

I own two pictures of God's throne room; one is based on Revelation 4 and the other on Isaiah 6:1–8. Both passages describe God's throne, but in Revelation John attempts more of the ineffable details: "At once I was in the Spirit, and there before me was a throne in heaven with someone sitting on it. And the one who sat there had the appearance of jasper and ruby. A rainbow that shone like an emerald encircled the throne. Surrounding the throne were twenty-four other thrones, and seated on them were twenty-four elders. They were dressed in white and had crowns of gold on their heads. From the throne came flashes of lightning, rumblings and peals of thunder. In front of the throne, seven lamps were blazing. These are the seven spirits of God. Also in front of the throne there was what looked like a sea of glass, clear as crystal" (vv. 2–6).

When I imagine this unbelievable sight, I see God seated high on the throne, controlling the lightning with a ruby face and surrounded by elders crying and shouting and singing and praising Him, their voices shaking every doorpost and threshold with words from Isaiah's vision:

> Holy, holy, holy is the LORD Almighty;
>   the whole earth is full of his glory.
>
> —ISAIAH 6:3

And John's vision:

> "Holy, holy, holy
> is the Lord God Almighty,"
> who was, and is, and is to come.
>
> —REVELATION 4:8

Four creatures are giving glory and honor and thanks to the one sitting on the throne who lives forever and ever into the future and even back for forever into the past. Isaiah and John describe a number and combination of wings and eyes that don't exist in our world. They saw something new. The twenty-four elders fall facedown, laying all their crowns before the throne.

And my Randy stood there.

Before Him.

And it will be the rest of my own life before I can understand. Was he trembling with fear? Will I?

What did God say to him?

What in the world will that conversation be like for me?

What will God ask? And what will I say—if I'm able to say anything?

The question that circles back to me, one that inspires more curiosity in my heart than God appearing like "jasper and ruby" or any of the other remarkable descriptions, is this: What will we experience in that moment?

I think two things happened in the moment that Randy stood before God.

First, my husband stood there fully known. Luke records Jesus saying to His followers, "For there is nothing hidden that will not be disclosed, and nothing concealed that will not be known or brought out into the open" (8:17). The author of Hebrews says likewise, "Nothing in all creation is hidden from God's sight. Everything is uncovered and laid bare before the eyes of him to whom we must give account" (4:13). Randy hid nothing; he wouldn't have been able to even if he wanted to. Every thought that crossed his mind, every word he ever said, every action he ever took, everything—even the things that Randy was able to hide from himself—was there, exposed before a perfect and holy and powerful God of justice. Amid the thunder and the praises and the sparkling sea of glass, Randy saw reality—the reality of who he was, the reality of who God is, and the reality of what had happened in his life. And of this I am convinced: in the moment of exposure, Randy felt more loved than he had ever felt in his entire life.

What's so fascinating is that this knowledge and this love were there all along. They weren't reserved for the moment Randy stood before Him. God always knew him like that (has always known us like that), and He always loved him like that (and loves us like that). It was just in that moment that Randy was able to see it for himself.

Second, God and Randy spoke. I think God asked Randy these questions—at least, this is how I've imagined the conversation going based on everything I know from Scripture:

God: "Did you love Me?"

There's a holy pause, and Randy answers. Then God speaks again.

God: "Did you love them?"

Randy answers again, in this throne room incapable of speaking anything but the absolute truth because nothing is hidden and everything has come to light. Randy knows the "them" that He is referring to is everyone he's ever met. Not just those who were easy to love. God's question is about love for the "least of these" (Matt. 25:40), the annoying people, Randy's enemies, his family, his friends, and everyone else.

"Did you love *them*?"

And since that moment became so very real for me, I've been turning these questions over in my mind. I won't know how Randy answered until I can ask him myself, but I can think about the way I want to respond. "Did you love Me? Did you love them?"

CONFIDENCE

Representations of the moment of judgment (even the word *judgment*—who likes that word?) can really scare people. I'm not here to do that. I give you full permission to be where you're at with this whole concept. Maybe we're saying or singing "Come, Lord Jesus!" but in our hidden hearts we're thinking, *But not yet because I'm not ready.* Maybe descriptions of God's power terrorize instead of inspire. This reaction is cultural, not biblical. Yes, it's going to be one overwhelming moment, but we don't have to wring our hands about it. Yes, Hebrews 4:13 explicitly declares, "Nothing in all creation is hidden in God's sight. Everything is uncovered and laid bare before the eyes of him to whom we must give account." But check out what comes next: "Therefore, since we have a great high priest who has ascended into heaven, Jesus the Son of God, let us hold firmly to the faith we profess. For we do not have a high priest who is unable to empathize with our weaknesses, but we have one who has been tempted in every way, just as we are—yet he did not sin" (vv. 14–15).

Yes, everything will be known. But we're not alone in the throne room. We have Jesus, who understands exactly how we feel. He knows more than what happened to us or what we did—He knows who we *are*. Totally. Completely. There's nothing left for us to explain because He already knows.

Then the author tells us how we can approach God's throne: "Let us then approach God's throne of grace with confidence" (v. 16).

Whaaat?!

We can approach God's throne of grace, with its jeweled brightness and the perpetual thunderstorm, the wild creatures singing "Holy, holy, holy," with *confidence?*

These verses used to mystify me. I couldn't identify with the attitude of confidence. When I imagined approaching a God in all His glory who knows absolutely everything I've ever done, the approach I imagined taking was not one of confidence. I figured some of the thoughts racing through my mind might be, *Did I do enough? Did I love enough? Was my amount of sin one of those, you know, "acceptable" amounts of sin?* Or maybe my thoughts would be a constant stream of *It's too late now, Megan!*

I thought of myself walking toward the throne with hesitancy, timidity, and insecurity.

And then Randy went first. Now, I see the moment differently. I had pictured it in my mind so many times, but the subject surveyed was no longer me—it was Randy, the person I loved the most in the whole world. Something important shifted. I imagined where—and on whom—Randy would have been lean-ing. And it was easier for me to see where grace broke through.

I've pictured this moment through the lens of someone I knew and deeply loved, and because of this, it's not hard for me to picture Jesus knowing and loving him even more. It's much easier to grasp the grace of God for someone else than it is to believe it for myself.

How can we approach Him confidently on that day?

Picture His throne: Holy. Indescribable—more splendor and strength than can be contained in one place. We've passed finite and we're into the infinite now.

Picture striding toward Him with confidence.

Why? You haven't earned it.

But you're not approaching God with your résumé of what you've done that makes you good enough to be there. If all you had to lean on was your résumé of spiritual disciplines, acts of service, and purposeful living, you wouldn't approach His throne with confidence. Randy wouldn't have either. None of us can. All of us have fallen short of the standard.

The standard we've fallen short of is the throne of God (a.k.a. the glory of God). I love the analogy from the Alpha study course: Picture a dot graph of all the world's people. At the top of the graph are dots representing all the best people, and at the bottom are all the worst. Hitler is at the bottom, Nelson Mandela and Corrie ten Boom are near the top, and so forth. We would all slot ourselves somewhere in between, and depending on where we land, we would be more or less happy with ourselves. But if we were to extend the top of the graph not just to the top of the page but to the sky, well, then the dots wouldn't seem all that far apart. When the standard is the glory of God, no one is even close.

But the author of Hebrews invites us to approach God's throne with confidence all the same. How? The only way we'll approach God's throne confidently is if we're holding Someone Else's résumé. "We wait for the blessed hope—the appearing of the glory of our great God and Savior, Jesus Christ, who gave himself for us to redeem us from all wickedness and to purify for himself a people that are his very own, eager to do what is good" (Titus 2:13–14).

So where can we lean?

On our only hope—on the one who gave Himself for us as an act of redemption.

That's where all the confidence comes from—His worth, not ours. His work, not ours. His righteousness, not ours. His cross, not ours.

"In Christ"

I learned at a young age that Jesus died on the cross for my sins. I learned that, by believing in Jesus, I could be saved from the eternal consequences of my sin: spiritual death, separation from God. What I didn't understand was what I received in the exchange.

The theological term is *double imputation*. We see it in 2 Corinthians 5:21: "God made him who had no sin to be sin for us." What this means is that the wages of our sin (as Rom. 6:23 states) is death. We deserve death because of sin. As a child, that made sense to me: sin = death. And death in Scripture simply means "separation." And accepting Jesus as my savior = life. God got rid of my sins. So how did God "get rid" of my sins? I kinda figured that He just ignored them.

I think that's what everyone figures. I did until I was deeply hurt and had to walk the road of forgiveness. I've started to realize that all true forgiveness is suffering. It's choosing to suffer on behalf of the person who wronged you so that they don't have to suffer. They rise as you endure. It's the opposite of ignoring;

it is a clear-eyed decision to face the suffering ourselves rather than an insistence on retribution.

So God doesn't ignore sin. He can't. He is not only all loving but also all just. As Creator, He has full comprehension of creation. Luke records the words of Jesus: "Are not five sparrows sold for two pennies? Yet not one of them is forgotten by God. Indeed, the very hairs of your head are all numbered. Don't be afraid; you are worth more than many sparrows" (12:6–7). God leaves nothing out. He doesn't ignore anything. It's not in His character. But, like Jesus said, we are worth so much to Him. So He had to do something about our sin and separation from Him. His character, His love, demanded it.

He couldn't ignore our sin, so on the cross He absorbed our sin. Jesus Christ, through His death on the cross, absorbed sin's curse and punishment so that we might go free. Sin had to be taken care of. In John's and Isaiah's visions of the throne, the angels and elders and creatures sing "Holy, holy, holy"—God is perfect in His holiness. Holiness and sin can't exist together. The consequence for sin was death. So Jesus came to us and died the death we deserved.

If we believe in Him, trusting that He came to us, lived the perfect life for us, and died the death we deserved, then we will be saved. He took that which we deserved, and we believe in Him. That is, we believe in His character, His goodness, His worthiness. We believe that He is more than enough to make up for our insufficiency. The gospel story—His birth (incarnation), death (as our atoning sacrifice), resurrection, ascension, and the gift of the Spirit—is the only thing stable enough to lean on. That's the only justification that can be accepted in the throne room. If we lean on this truth, we are saved from the consequence of our sin (eternal separation from the one who is "holy, holy, holy"). As Paul wrote to the Corinthians, "God made him who had no sin to be sin for us, so that in him we might become the righteousness of God" (2 Cor. 5:21). We stand before God fully forgiven for all of it.

All of it.

Let me say it again, because some of you think I'm referring only to the socially acceptable sins, like being dishonest that one time or being a tad too prideful. No. You're forgiven for the abortion, sexual immorality, pornography, alcohol/pill/drug addiction as you stand before God because Christ went to the cross and paid it all. Leaning on His atoning sacrifice on the cross, you will stand before God fully forgiven for all of it. You cannot and have not and will not out-sin the cross.

But I said imputation was double. The first part: Jesus took that which you deserved. He bore the consequence—for all sin—for all time. But there's a second half to that verse, the second part of the double imputation. Let's look at 2 Corinthians 5:21 again: "God made him who had no sin to be sin for us, *so that in him* we might become the righteousness of God" (emphasis added). In Him, we're fully forgiven, but it doesn't stop there. By grace (unmerited/unearned favor on our lives) through faith (and trust not in ourselves but in Him and His life, death, and resurrection), we receive that which He deserved. He took that which we deserved, and we receive that which He deserved. He takes ours; we take His. In Christ, we're both fully forgiven *and* fully accepted.

Imputed righteousness is a concept in Christian theology stating that the righteousness of Christ (the position of being right with God) is imputed, or treated as if it were ours, through faith. I've heard justification before God defined as "just as if I hadn't done anything." This doesn't do justice to what justification is. The result is not the same as if I had not done anything. That would be pure innocence. Justification is fuller and richer and costlier than that. We have done something, and Christ paid an infinite amount of suffering for that something we did and will do. And we receive that unfathomable gift of love and sacrifice with undying gratitude and full knowledge of what it cost Jesus on our behalf. While we wish we could skip over all the pain of life, know this: the glories of heaven will mean so much more after we've experienced the opposite—after we've seen the ramifications of our rebellion toward God. The beauty and glory and perfection of heaven mean more because we've gone through this life first.

Many of us think the way forgiveness works is that God chooses not to see, when it's the opposite. He chooses to fully see. He fully sees us and fully sees Jesus.

See the difference?

As we approach God's throne, we don't lean on our own résumés of what makes us a pretty good person. We lean on His résumé. We reach deep into the pocket of our souls and pull out our right standing in Christ.

I imagine my approach to the throne differently now. The splendor and the might and the majesty are there, but I keep my eyes fixed on His face. I'm totally known. Everything except for where I was really leaning has been stripped away. And then we speak.

God: "Did you love Me?"

Me: "Yes!"

God (smiling): "Did you love them?"

Me, answering honestly and freely and almost humorously: "Sometimes."

In that moment, all I will be able to do is lean on Christ. I am in Him and He is in me: "I plead the blood of a substitute. I believe in Jesus." And that will be more than enough.

Where can we lean? We can lean on Him—our high priest.

Our substitute. Our hope of salvation. Heaven is full of people like us, people who know they don't deserve to be there. People like Randy, who held Another's résumé in their hands when they met God face-to-face. It's only by the blood of Christ as we lean on Him, putting our full weight not on ourselves and our résumés but standing bare before God, fully exposing who we truly are at the core in Christ, that we are admitted. In Him, we've never been more loved.

GO TO GOD

Someday Soon

Preparation is important to me. I like being ready for what's happening next.

We know we'll stand before God one day, even though we don't know when that moment will come. This is something that we can relax about too—yes, even our deaths! I'm not trying to be morbid, I'm just stating what we already know: this life will end, for every single one of us. And then we'll stand before His throne.

Take a moment to think through that conversation, as if it was going to happen soon. Of course, I don't know for sure what God will ask us, but I think it will have something to do with Jesus' greatest commandments. Did you love God, and did you love others?

Right now, what feelings and thoughts come to you when you think about appearing before God? Share them with God. (If you wish, write them in the following space.)

What would you say if He asked if you loved Him? Don't just think through this on your own—tell Him.

What would you say if He asked if you loved others? You can be honest. God is not surprised by the truth.

End by thanking God for salvation through Christ. If you are not confident that you are in Christ, you can respond to the gift of grace and salvation by praying this prayer. It's not just about the words spoken but about the genuine faith and personal conviction behind them:

> *Jesus, I confess that I am a sinner in need of Your forgiveness. I believe that You are the Son of God and that You died on the cross for my sins. I repent of (turn from) my sins and ask You for your forgiveness.*
>
> *Please come into my life, be my Lord and Savior, and guide me in Your path of righteousness. I place all my trust in You and Your grace for my eternal salvation.*
>
> *Thank You for Your love and gift of eternal life.*
>
> *I pray all this in the power of your name, amen.*

If you prayed this prayer, welcome to the family of God. Next to grace, I'm convinced that one of God's best gifts to us is one another. Seek fellowship within a Christian community to encourage you and walk with you in your new relationship with Jesus Christ.

3
PART

In All Your Ways
Submit to Him

CHAPTER 6

GRIEF

Trust in the LORD with all your heart
and lean not on your own understanding;
in all your ways submit to him,
and he will make your paths straight.

BEFORE WE GET into this chapter, let me introduce this third part of the book. So far, we've walked through each of the phrases of our key verses one chapter at a time. The pace is going to change now. We are going to spend six chapters on seven words: "In all your ways submit to him." We're going to explore that one phrase by talking through some "ways" from my own life.

Just to recap, in the past few years, my family structure shifted radically. I lost my husband. My boys have grown out of diapers, but they're still little. I've been traveling and teaching and raising my sons, and all the while, I've been grieving my best friend and partner. The way I approach everything—from yard maintenance to parenting to spending money—had to change.

I was thinking about ways, or areas of my life, that have been hard to hand over to God—not because I don't want to but because I feel like I don't even know how to start doing that. Is it something I do once? Or daily? What does submitting to Him in all my ways look like on the practical level? I don't want to hold back here; I don't want to give you a bunch of spiritual success stories. I want you to know how things have actually been. These chapters let you in on the places I've been struggling with trusting Him. Here are the ways that surfaced and became this third part of the book: grief, trials, risk, friendships, money, and mistakes.

I'll bet there's some overlap between us—in some of those areas, you're not sure how to submit to God either—but my ways might not be your big ones. I'll tell you about my ways.

HOUSE OF MOURNING

Early on February 21, 2021, I sneaked into my son's bedroom. There was not a good way to tell him, but he had to know. I curled around his tiny body and said with a broken voice, "Something happened last night that will change our lives forever."

Since my husband, Randy, went to heaven that morning, my boys and I have been grieving. As I've lived grief, day in and day out, for the past few years, I've started to see that grief is another one of the "ways" of life that can be submitted to God. In grief—and in all my other ways—He doesn't want me to be alone. I'm not saying this has come naturally to any of us who loved Randy and were loved by him. But we started to see the truth in Ecclesiastes 7:2: "It is better to go to a house of mourning than to go to a house of feasting, for death is the destiny of everyone; the living should take this to heart." We— Randy's parents and brother, me, the boys, and our family and friends—found ourselves in that house of mourning, and it was better. Did it always feel better? No. Absolutely not. But it made us consider how we wanted to live the rest of our lives. Randy's death has led all of us into this new depth of longing for heaven and longing for Jesus, this realization that yes, one day, we too will die. I've found gratitude in that house of mourning, a kind of gratitude I hadn't realized existed. But don't get me wrong, I still hate being there.

While we live, we grieve, and I don't know if that will ever change. Part of being human in a broken world is loss and grief. This is a consequence of our willful rebellion against our creator, a painful, powerful, and palpable reminder of what going our own way—that autonomy we thought we wanted—really costs us. The hope that we will one day be resurrected in Jesus, as beautiful and real as it is, doesn't negate the pain of the loss, nor should it. I've found gifts amid the hell of pain, but the pain itself is not a gift. The by-products of enduring it with God are. In 1 Thessalonians 4, Paul teaches that it's okay for Christians to grieve. We just do it differently from everyone else. We do it with hope. We have hope that although this world is not as it was supposed to be, it won't always be this way. Grieving with hope, I think, is what it means for me to "acknowledge Him" (that's the verb from the NASB) in my ways of grief. It's not as it should be (so grieve); it won't always be this way (have hope). That's what I'm trying to learn.

One thing that's come up for me as I've been on this journey of learning to give myself to God in my grief is how I invite other people into my grief. As I've talked about grief with my friends and spoken about grief at churches and written about grief, I've started asking God, "Are You inviting me to share about pain or to show it?"

It seems like He's asking me to show it more than He's asking me to share about it. This chapter—all the chapters in this book, but this one especially—is written out of the pain of

Randy's absence. I want to do three things with this chapter: help you recognize what grief is, tell you why grief is important, and show you how to grieve well.

What Grief Is

Let's start with Scripture. In Romans 8:18–27, Paul writes about grief, ranging from the cosmic to the intensely personal. Since the fall—the moment when Adam and Eve betrayed God and sin entered the world (Genesis 3)—all creation has been in a state of mourning. Sin never shows up alone, but our sin dragged death into the world with it. Paul goes so far as to say that, as a result of sin, the world is in "bondage to decay." And each of us experiences this cosmic grief on personal levels. Individuals also grieve deeply. The experience of that kind of pain defies even our ability to use words. We're all reduced to groans; speech doesn't suffice for creation, for us, or for God Himself.

I consider that our present sufferings are not worth comparing with the glory that will be revealed in us. For the creation waits in eager expectation for the children of God to be revealed. For the creation was subjected to frustration, not by its own choice, but by the will of the one who subjected it, in hope that the creation itself will be liberated from its bondage to decay and brought into the freedom and glory of the children of God.

We know that *the whole creation has been groaning* as in the pains of childbirth right up to the present time. Not only so, *but we ourselves, who have the firstfruits of the Spirit, groan inwardly as we wait eagerly for our adoption to sonship, the redemption of our bodies.* For in this hope we were saved. But hope that is seen is no hope at all. Who hopes for what they already have? But if we hope for what we do not yet have, we wait for it patiently.

In the same way, the Spirit helps us in our weakness. We do not know what we ought to pray for, but the Spirit himself intercedes for us *through wordless groans*. And he who searches our hearts knows the mind of the Spirit, because the Spirit intercedes for God's people in accordance with the will of God. (Emphases added)

Paul writes, "Who hopes for what they already have?" Grief is the recognition that something is not as it should be—something pivotal is missing. My four-year-old throws tantrums when we stop doing something fun or leave friends, in part because, somewhere down in his little soul, he knows that these moments of delight and friendship and sheer joy were never supposed to end in the first place. And in this way, part of grief can be an unexpected and complex blessing because it invites us to experience reality.

Grief invites us to consider the world. It's an opportunity to think about the reality we experience daily and long for a day when all will be as it should be. Is this world, with death and pain and suffering, as it should be? No. It isn't. We know that things aren't right somehow. This isn't how it should be. This is not the best of all possible worlds. The act of grieving is both an appropriate response to a world that is out of alignment with God's original design and a longing for the day when the world will be made right again.

Grief is not just normal, it's necessary.

I didn't pray with words for the first two weeks. I didn't know what I was supposed to say to God. My heart couldn't speak a coherent sentence. I trusted that the Spirit was praying for me with groans, like Paul says in Romans 8, because that was all I had. I remember being so gutted, being physically held by people who loved me as I yelled because I had to do something with all that pain. I hadn't slept. After a few days, I finally was able to fall asleep, and later I found out why. My friend Mandy had asked the Lord if she could somehow carry the pain for me. I'm convinced God answered her prayer. She didn't sleep that night, but I did.

In the years since, I've talked through the pain. I've gone back to the moment with a therapist. I've ignored the pain, only to find it even more acute when it explodes out in the context of a seemingly small annoyance.

Grief is a mess.

Elisabeth Kübler-Ross and David Kessler wrote a book called *On Grief and Grieving*, which articulated the "five stages of grief." I've weaved in and out of all of these. I don't know if you've grieved hard yet. But if you haven't, you're going to. You're going to lose something—or someone—precious. And your thoughts and feelings will probably circle in patterns of denial, anger, bargaining, depression, and acceptance.[16] The experience of grief is nonlinear, but I've found that having some markers in the jungle is helpful.

I call denial the "I just can't believe it" stage. And truthfully, I've been grateful for it. Sometimes, I just can't take the weight of believing it, and so, for a moment, I don't. I can remember when I was the angriest. It was the same moment I was the most depressed. I thought, *Randy is somewhere better now, but we're still here. How could he do something like that to us?* No, he didn't choose to leave, but still, he was gone. It was somewhat irrational of me, but I'm thankful that, in grief, you can be irrational.

In bargaining, I'd pester God with the phrase "If only . . ." I'm still coming up with phrases that start with "If only." I'm not sure how I feel about the word *acceptance* in this sequence— the idea that, somehow, you'll make it to a "new normal." My friend Sue Beanie says, "It's not a new normal, it's just a new different." Yeah, I'm not sure we'll make it back to normal, but I do have hope that we're going somewhere. After *On Grief and Grieving* came out, one of the authors, David Kessler, lost his son. He came back to the publishers with the idea for a sixth stage: meaning.[17]

At first, I felt uncomfortable with the idea of finding meaning in Randy's death. Thankfully, Kessler didn't mean that we need to find a meaningful answer to "Why?" that makes the pain feel almost worth it. That's impossible. This is what so many Christians want to do in the face of suffering and loss. They try to look for an answer why, and the results are all sorts of crazy. "Maybe God needed him in heaven more than we needed him here." *What?* "Someday I'll understand why this happened." *Probably not.* "We should be happy because she is in a better place." *But what if I can't just "be happy"?*

Kessler was not trying to find a meaningful answer. Rather, he was referencing the opportunity to make meaning in response to the present moment because it is all we have. Have meaningful conversations. Talk about meaningful things. Make meaning. I've tried to create meaning with my grief.

I'm trusting that this is meaningful for you. I would not write about grief otherwise.

WHY GRIEF IS IMPORTANT

"What would I have done if I couldn't have grieved?"

I asked my dad this question when we were sitting in a Chick-fil-A, watching my boys tear around the play area. I honestly don't know what I would have done if God had not given me grief.

Let me ask you this question: Have you let yourself feel the pain?

Because grief is a door into something I know God wants for you: Himself.

He's the reward.

Not heaven but Him.

God desires that we desire Him. Heaven is not the goal, it's the place we get to experience God. And I have never longed for God and more of what He longs for like this. I'm longing for peace. Deep, unaffected, untainted peace and delight. I look forward to laughter. I love laughing. Everything in me wants to see Randy again. But I know that my deepest longing is for someone of whom Randy was an image bearer: Jesus.

I've never wanted this more in my entire life, and it's because of my grief. It has drawn me to Him. I needed grief, and I think you do too. In his book *Holy Longing*, Ronald Rolheiser writes,

> What we have dreamed for our lives can never be. Thus we have a choice: We can spend the rest of our lives angry, trying to protect ourselves against something that has already happened to us, death and unfairness, or we can grieve our losses, abuses, and deaths and, through that, eventually attain the joy and delights that are in fact possible for us.
>
> Alice Miller states this all in psychological language, but the choice is really a paschal one. We face many deaths within our lives and the choice is ours as to whether those deaths will be terminal (snuffing out life and spirit) or whether they will be paschal (opening us to new life and spirit). Grieving is the key to the latter.[18]

There have been dark, hollow times when I've leaned toward the terminal. How could anything good come from this? I have to say "my *late* husband," and I'm in my thirties. I haven't gotten used to that. Maybe I never will. But, because of God's mercy, I have experienced new life through grief too. I'm longing for God like I've never longed for Him. My boys and I have been lifted up in prayer and materially provided for. We've seen miracles. Our grief has opened us up to new life and spirit.

But even though this is true, it's difficult to want grief. I can see everything that God has brought into my life through grief and still not want it. It's a gift I never asked for. Even now, I tend toward wanting relief over grief.

I'll admit something embarrassing. I tried to make a grieving friend laugh while I was working on these thoughts. I'm serious. I was writing about grief, she walked into my office while grieving, and instead of just being present, of bearing witness to her sadness, I tried to shoo it away with a joke.

Here's some good news: God doesn't ever shoo away our pain.

It's not that He doesn't want relief for us; He just has greater plans for our pain. He wants us to get to relief, but eventually. In grief, we become more like Him. In our sorrow, we comfort others. We "get it" in ways that nobody else can. As we comfort, we find ourselves comforted too. God draws those who grieve closer to Him. "Blessed are those who mourn," Jesus promised, "for they will be comforted" (Matt. 5:4). Before the relief, He brings purpose to the pain. Second Corinthians 1:3–5 says, "Praise be to the God and Father of our Lord Jesus Christ, the Father of compassion and the God of all comfort, who comforts us in all our troubles, so that we can comfort those in any trouble with the comfort we ourselves receive from God. For just as we share abundantly in the sufferings of Christ, so also our comfort abounds through Christ."

We want to be plucked out of the pain, but God wants to be present with us in it.

If we don't grieve, we'll look for relief somewhere else, and there's a whole host of unhealthy options. Or we'll get stuck at the stage we're in and we'll keep reacting to everyone based on being stuck in depression, denial, or anger. The truth is that we can't heal what we are unwilling to feel. If we don't acknowledge Him in our grief, we'll live out of the stage we're stuck in.

I like the idea that grief is the antidote to trauma. It's the healthy response to loss. Trauma leaves us feeling stuck. Grief has the power to move us. Either downward into our hearts or upward to lament with God, and then ideally outward toward others as we allow them to carry our burden alongside us. Many shy away from grief, fearing it traps us, but avoiding grief is what keeps us truly stuck.

So talk about it. Even if it feels like you're talking about the same thing over and over. God moves us as we talk about it. Research continually suggests that discussing trauma and grief is critical to healing and growing through it. James Pennebaker's groundbreaking studies on the importance of talking about trauma reveal that expressive writing and verbal processing can lead to significant psychological and physical benefits, including improved emotional processing, reduced distress, enhanced immune system function, and greater overall well-being.[19]

For the first year, all I could do was receive. I felt uncomfortable because my days were spent receiving love rather than giving love away. Everything felt backward. The only thing I felt like I was sharing with anyone or giving to anyone was my pain. Thankfully, my sister, Kimi, reminded me that processing pain wasn't just for me, it also brought out the best in her as she sacrificially loved and comforted me. Submitting to God in grief meant opening up the grief and letting God use others. Eventually, I did start to give to others again. And it was different from how it had been before. I felt the words of Paul's greeting in 2 Corinthians deeply: I could "comfort those in any trouble" with the comfort I myself receive from God. If you're willing to go there with Him, if you're willing to grieve, He will use the pain you've been carrying or maybe ignoring.

How to Grieve Well

In the months after Randy died, I was handed this verse more times than I can remember: "The Lord is close to the broken-hearted and saves those who are crushed in spirit" (Ps. 34:18). I clung to that verse. And I realized this: It's not just that God's nearness brings comfort. He's not just "near." He is grieving too. My favorite person to grieve with was my sister; when I grieved, she grieved too. Likewise, as we grieve, we join God *in His grief.*

When you talk about grief with God, you're talking to someone who understands and is well acquainted with it (Isa. 53:3). One of Jesus' epithets in the books of prophecy is "man of sorrows" (Isa. 53:3 ESV).

In John 11, Jesus' deep grief is on display. His friend Lazarus, the brother of Martha and Mary, is gravely ill. The sisters send Jesus a message: "Lord, the one you love is sick" (v. 3). He waits for days before arriving in their town of Bethany. He isn't far. But He does wait. While He waits, Lazarus dies. And, understandably, the sisters don't understand.

"If you had been here, my brother would not have died," Martha tells Him (v. 21). Mary waits to come see Him until He asks for her. She falls at His feet and says the same thing.

Where were You?

I don't know their tone, but I know what mine was when I asked Him the same question.

Jesus asks to see where they laid His friend. He's taken there, and then He weeps. Did you ever memorize John 11:35, the shortest verse in the Bible? "Jesus wept." I used to wonder why He cried. Why cry when you know what's going to happen? He grieved before He raised Lazarus. He could've raised him upon arrival, in those moments with his sisters, and bypassed the pain of grief. But He knew we would need a tool for the moment we faced death on this earth. He had the power to raise his friend right then and there, but instead of taking a shortcut away from tears, Jesus modeled for us what to do when we face death: grieve.

Jesus, who never sinned, grieved because there's nothing wrong with grief. He was perfect, mature, full of faith and hope and love, and He grieved. I'm struck by the range of emotion we see from Jesus in His grief. When John says that Jesus was "deeply moved" (v. 33), the word there means angry, like enraged. It's not just that Jesus was sad but that He, too, felt deeply the wrongness of death. He was practiced in grief. He could face it without flinching. He could let Himself weep. This prepared Him for the depth of sorrow He experienced in His passion. In the garden of Gethsemane, He grieved. In Matthew 26:38, He said to His closest followers, "My soul is overwhelmed with sorrow to the point of death. Stay here and keep watch with me." Luke 22:44 says, "And being in anguish, he prayed more earnestly, and his sweat was like drops of blood falling to the ground." On the cross, He lamented in the words of the psalmist: "My God, my God, why have you forsaken me?" (Matt. 27:46).

Jesus grieved deeply because He loves deeply.

His grief and our grief are expressions of hope.

Grief and hope are God's tools for living in a fallen, broken world. Some Christians suppress grief because they think it isn't an expression of hope, but it is. Things are not supposed to be this way. Grief inherently expresses the hope that things are supposed to be different. As Tim Keller is often attributed with having said, "The opposite of joy is not sadness, it's hopelessness." If we had no hope, we'd feel the dullness of apathy instead of the sharp pangs of grief.

But, out of hope, we can question His timing.

We can get angry with His ways.

We can even fling ourselves to the ground.

Hope compels us to ask God audacious questions in anger and desperation, questions like "God, how long?" And God, in His mercy, moves with us through these feelings. We don't have to hide any way that we grieve from God; we can submit all our ways to Him. Our confused ways, sad ways, irrational ways, and angry ways.

We trust the promise that we won't have to wait forever.

Sin and death are not forever because Jesus is coming back. In Revelation 21:1–5, John describes his incredible vision of heaven and earth coming together. This isn't just a happy ending—this is God's long-fought victory. But for our suffering in this life, this passage wouldn't carry the same weight or meaning. That's why our grief is necessary. It allows us to feel the weight of our sin and rebellion as the price for walking away from God. It acknowledges the important truth that the only solution to both our grief and our rebellion is God.

That's why God didn't just move from the garden of Eden into paradise. We needed this.

But John describes what's going to happen next:

> Then I saw "a new heaven and a new earth," for the first heaven and the first earth had passed away, and there was no longer any sea. I saw the Holy City, the new Jerusalem, coming down out of heaven from God, prepared as a bride beautifully dressed for her husband. And I heard a loud voice from the throne saying, "Look! God's dwelling place is now among the people, and he will dwell with them. They will be his people, and God himself will be with them and be their God. 'He will wipe every tear from their eyes. There will be no more death' or mourning or crying or pain, for the old order of things has passed away."
>
> He who was seated on the throne said, "I am making everything new!"

Grief is evidence of this reality: we are still separated from our God. It was never meant to be that way. And yes, friend, that separation hurts to the core. Death is one of the sharpest reminders that the separation will not last forever. God's dwelling place—His home—will be with us. Death will be nothing but a memory. It will never hurt us again. Every tear in the meantime is significant. Every tear is aligning our hearts with His. There will be no more death, or mourning, or crying, or pain. A pastor I heard, Kyle Idleman, wondered whether the author of Revelation felt that human language didn't have the capacity to describe what heaven will be like, so he created a note in his iPhone to join John in dreaming of what *won't* be there. This is what theologians refer to as "apophatic theology"—defining something ineffable by focusing on what it is not. This is necessary when it comes to God. In many ways, this is the only way we can come to meaningful clarity. So I created a note in my phone, too, not one full of what heaven will be like but one full of what will be "no more." In heaven, there will be no more:

- Death
- Mourning
- Crying
- Pain
- Cancer
- Affairs
- Anxiety
- Heart disease
- Cerebral palsy
- CPAP machines
- Foster care
- Prescriptions
- Worry
- Divorce
- Rejection
- Loneliness
- Feeling left out
- Laundry (well, I'm not sure about laundry)
- Self-consciousness
- Apathy
- Arguments
- Suffering
- Longing
- Fear
- Depression
- Hurry—because we will be relaxed

No more:

- Family dysfunction
- Wheelchairs
- Abuse
- Nightmares
- Radiation and chemo
- Racism
- Middle of the night phone calls
- Self-hate

- Sexual abuse
- Eating disorders
- Comparison
- Failure
- Breakups
- Acne
- Suicide
- Sin
- Hope

Wait, what?

Yep! There will be no more hope. As my friend Jeff Carter once said, "Heaven will be the absence of hope—not in the sense of hopelessness, but in the sense of completion and fulfillment. There will no longer be a need for hope. Hope is what drives us to look to heaven as our actual home. When we arrive home, we will be complete. We will have peace. We will be with God—which is the ache of every human heart. But until then God has given us this incredible gift called hope."

No more:

- Dissatisfaction
- Burdens
- Pornography
- Alcoholism
- Wrinkles
- Muffin tops
- Angry neighbors
- Persecution
- Welfare
- Glasses

- Dead grass
- Browning plants
- Single parenting
- Prosthetics
- Disability
- Funeral homes
- Nursing homes
- Waiting rooms
- Double chins
- Shaving

- Traffic
- Hormones
- Dieting
- Shame
- Blame
- Hiding
- Condemnation

- Accusations
- Fear of the future
- Heart attacks
- Gossip
- Sadness
- Badness
- Grief

"He who was seated on the throne said, 'I am making everything new!'"

Do you long for this?

Are you letting yourself long for this?

To let yourself long for this is to grieve that it's "not yet."

Everything will be new.

Our faith will be sight because life will be as it should be, and we will be face to face with Jesus at a never-ending feast. It's going to be a wedding, not a funeral, one day.

There will be peace.

And laughter.

Until then, we grieve.

And if you've experienced significant loss or feel deeply the brokenness of the world, can I encourage you to do just that? Grieve deeply, as Jesus did. Don't avoid those feelings. If you do avoid them, they will consume you. Grief will not be denied. We must open up how we feel to God and others. If you feel it and let those feelings lead you downward and upward and outward, you will find that your grief can be transformative, even useful. I guess what I'm saying is, if you need to, friends, grieve with me. Acknowledge God in your grief and you'll find that He is grieving too. You'll find Him the deeper you go in yours. And one day, grief will be no more.

Longing for the Day

Let's go to God with our grief.

Take a moment now to open your heart to Him.

First, recall a time when you grieved.

It doesn't have to be a big thing—sometimes we need to practice with the "little" things, and then we find out how not-so-little they are. Maybe it's the loss of a friendship that mattered to you, or the loss of a job that brought you a sense of purpose, or the loss of a marriage, or even the loss of a dream you had for your life.

Do you have a moment or a circumstance in your mind?

Whatever it may be, bring it to God with honesty and vulnerability.

"The act of grieving is both an appropriate response to a world that is out of alignment with God's original design and a longing for the day when the world will be made right again."

Go to God with how that grief is tied to an aspect of our world being out of alignment with His original design.

Go to God with your longing for a day when this aspect of our world will be made right again. Imagine Him grieving and longing with you—because He is.

Is there anything you haven't let yourself grieve? Tell Him about it now. If you can use only one or two words to describe it, that's fine. Let Him in.

Now thank Him for the experience of grief. Thank Him that He grieves with you. Thank Him for the hope that it won't always be this way.

CHAPTER 7

TRIALS

Trust in the LORD with all your heart
and lean not on your own understanding;
*in **all your ways** submit to him,*
and he will make your paths straight.

WHO DOESN'T LOVE the movie *The Sandlot*?

Well, my friend Tony doesn't. One character ruined it for him.

The movie begins with a family moving to a new town at the beginning of summer. This is a problem, of course, because the young son in the family doesn't have friends to enjoy the summer with. Noticing this, the mom urges the stepdad to get out and play catch with his stepson. He's hesitant as he has other work to do. She urges him, he complies, and they begin playing catch, and the young boy is terrible at baseball. He can't catch. He can't even throw the ball. The stepdad gives a few quick pointers, but the kid merits nothing except disappointment. This familial experiment ends with the stepson taking a baseball to the face and the stepdad giving up.

But don't worry, the neighborhood baseball star, Benny Rodriguez, befriends the young boy and invites him to the sandlot. The boy proves there that he is still not good at baseball, and the other young boys wonder why the baseball star even invited this kid in the first place. Benny believes in his newfound neighbor friend and sets him up for his first big catch of the movie. And the adventures begin. The boy learns to play baseball, makes new friends, and has a few incidents with a giant neighborhood dog and the lifeguard Wendy Peffercorn. The main plotline has the boy swiping his stepdad's prized baseball (signed by Babe Ruth) and hitting his first home run with it. From there, the boys go on a journey to retrieve the ball. Eventually, they get it back from the dog and make friends with the scary neighbor who turns out to be not so scary. The end. As far as movies go, it's pretty victorious.

So why doesn't my friend Tony like the movie? He doesn't like the stepdad. The stepdad is uninterested in teaching his stepson anything. He doesn't have patience. He only has quick pointers and unmet expectations.

The movie ends with what feels like a heroic moment. After the incident with the prized baseball and the dog is resolved, the movie cuts to the boy playing catch again with his stepdad. This time they're both smiling. This time they're enjoying the moment. This time the boy is miraculously athletic. There's even heroic music to go with it. But something is off here. The stepdad missed out on the relationship. He missed out on the adventure. He wanted to play baseball only once the kid had figured it out on his own.

Ouch.

Can you imagine that kind of pressure?

Unfortunately, some of you probably can.

This is the opposite of how our heavenly Father works with us. He's not waiting for us to "get it" on our own. He's not expecting us to know everything or even be quick to learn anything on our own. He's in for the journey, not encouraging autonomy. He's not like the stepdad. He's more like Benny, the true hero, the one who invites the boy on a journey, sets him up to make catches, encourages him in his weaknesses, and ends up taking the entire burden on himself to snag the ball away from the dog.

God is not waiting for you to figure it all out before He connects with you. You don't have to figure out prayer or Scripture first. If you want to you can pause in the middle of this paragraph and just be with Him. But often, we don't pause. And we shy away from being with Him. Why is that? Because although we know God isn't like the stepdad from *The Sandlot*, we sure live like He is. We hear that good sermon preaching the ideal (how we're supposed to be living), and we do our best on our own to shrink the gap between where we're currently at and how we "should" be living. And when we fall short, rather than landing on grace, we land in shame, which leads us even farther away from relationship with God.

Our heavenly Father is taking us on a journey and inviting us to play a little catch. If you don't catch it all, that's okay. He's not interested in your figuring it out by yourself or waiting for the perfect friend to come along, He's interested in teaching you at your pace. And He's using everything (misses, catches, run-ins with the neighborhood dog, friends) to mature you so that you don't lack a thing in the end. Doesn't that sound good? It *is* good, but like our hero from *The Sandlot*, we may be surprised by the intensity of the adventure that takes us to that place.

NOT LACKING ANYTHING

To understand the type of journey God wants to take us on, let's start with Scripture. We're going to look at the beginning of the only letter written by James. James was the half brother of Jesus. Same mom, different dad. His letter is distinct in the New Testament as its wisdom literature. Wisdom literature was common in the Old Testament (Psalms, Proverbs, etc.) but the clearest example of wisdom literature in the New Testament is found in the book of James. James is sometimes called the "Proverbs of the New Testament." In his letter he offers wisdom for living out our Christian faith and writes to people who know life is hard. He begins by introducing himself and those he is writing to. And then he offers some pretty startling wisdom: "James, a servant of God and of the Lord Jesus Christ, to the twelve tribes scattered among the nations: Greetings. Consider it pure joy, my brothers and sisters, whenever you face trials of many kinds, because you know that the testing of your faith produces perseverance. Let perseverance finish its work so that you may be mature and complete, *not lacking anything*" (1:1–4, emphasis added).

In addressing his letter to "the twelve tribes scattered among the nations," James is clearly writing about trials to people who are facing them, but the advice he gives isn't what they expected to hear. He offers them a new perspective on trials. James makes this link between trials and joy, which at first seems like an infuriating paradox but is actually something we can experience in our lives all the time.

Not so conveniently, my wonderful late husband was born on Father's Day. Every year, right around Father's Day, it's going to be Randy's birthday. This confluence of holidays isn't going to get easier for me and my boys, but it is the way it is. This past year, on the Saturday between Randy's birthday (Friday) and Father's Day (Sunday), I picked up the passage of Scripture I would be teaching a few weeks later: James 1:2. "Consider it pure joy, my brothers and sisters, whenever you face trials of many kinds." What?!

Pure joy?!

I was right in the middle of a trial, and I wouldn't have immediately thought to consider it pure joy.

But as I thought about it, I realized something. James is not saying, "Look at the trial and feel happy." No! He knows that the visceral emotion partnered with trials is sorrow, not joy. But he says, "Consider it pure joy." He's referencing the intensity, not the exclusivity, of the joy. He is not saying, "Have only joy." He's saying, "Have the fullness of joy too." Intensity, not exclusivity. This is important. He's inviting those suffering to consider trials from a new perspective. First, see the hard, have sorrow, yes, of course. This has to the be the case; otherwise, we would be something less than human. The Psalms teach us this lesson beautifully and poignantly. They are filled with examples of people realistically facing their suffering with deep faith and worship, through lament and anger. Worship doesn't somehow obliterate suffering. Instead, suffering becomes a vehicle for transformative worship, or maybe better, it becomes the sacrifice the psalmist brings in worship. We have to be aware of our visceral emotions in trials. But we also have to consider the trials from another perspective: the fullness of joy—heaven.

Each time I consider Randy and heaven and Jesus, my perspective shifts.

When I prepare a message in my own strength with my own interests in mind, I think about how it (and I) will be received. But when I consider a heavenly perspective, my process changes. My whole focus changes. I don't care about how I'm going to be received anymore, I just want people to be received into heaven. I want to make sure people know the truth that sets them eternally free.

When I think about heaven, I worry less about what people think of me.

When I think about heaven, I think of the hope of a day when tears won't be necessary and death will be no more.

When I think about heaven, I think more of loving others than finding love myself.

When I think about heaven, I think more of what God values: kindness over comparison, celebration over envy, reconciliation over being right, eternal treasure over material toys, listening over needing to be heard, and love over self-consciousness.

When I think about heaven, I start to understand what James says about "not lacking anything." It's all going to be there.

When I think about heaven and consider trials, I realize that trials aren't meaningless. If the one we follow went through the greatest trials and pain possible, He wouldn't just allow us to go through our trials without a greater purpose as well. No wonder Jesus sent His half brother to write a letter to those "scattered" and suffering. And James gets right to it in the letter: "Greetings. Okay, so when you face trials, consider joy." He knew you would consider sadness. He knew you would consider grief. He knew you'd get angry. He offers another perspective: "Consider it pure (intense, overwhelming) joy *whenever* you face trials of many kinds." *When*ever, not *if* ever. James knew that trials are inevitable. Do you? People often refer to this as having a "theology of suffering." I kind of hate how common suffering is, but it's the reality of life in this world, and James can help us make sense of it.

THEOLOGY OF SUFFERING

James gives us a perspective to consider in our trials. Sorrow—yes. Also, joy! Why? "Because you know that the testing of your faith produces perseverance. Let perseverance finish its work so that you may be mature and complete, not lacking anything" (1:3–4). James is offering the potential of trials. Notice, I didn't say the *guarantee* of trials. Trials are an opportunity, not an outcome. The outcome is determined by what we do with the opportunity. This reminds me of the classic "aircraft attitude" analogy. The attitude of an airplane is the positioning of the nose relative to the horizon. A negative attitude means the plane is pointed down; positive means it's pointed up. When the headwind kicks up, the attitude of the plane will determine whether it crashes or soars.

Trials either make you (and your faith) better or they make you bitter. We've seen this, right? Trials either mature you, make you able to help and understand other people, or they make you more self-absorbed and obsessed with your problems, which, by the way, is human. "You know that the testing of your faith produces perseverance." Do you know this? I'm only beginning to understand it.

I recently did what's called a "life map." I took sticky notes and spent an hour jotting down each moment, person, book, circumstance, job, situation that had a positive effect on my life—one per sticky note. Then I spent a second hour writing down each moment, relationship, etc. that was a moment of pain in my life on a different-colored sticky note. I was so into this activity I even invited my parents to have lunch that day so we could recount memories I may have forgotten. After each sixty-minute segment, I waited on the Holy Spirit to bring even more memories to mind that He knew were significant. The next hour was spent putting them in chronological order. From there, I grouped the moments into chapters and wrote my logical and illogical learnings (e.g., friendships cannot define you, adults are trustworthy [or not], I have to protect myself). I learned a lot. Primarily, though, I learned two things:

1. Success is limited in its ability to grow you.
2. Trials have the potential to grow you, mature you, and strengthen your faith and endurance in life.

I know trials make you feel weak, but in truth, they have the potential to make you much stronger than success can.

God changes you during your trials. Consider what Solomon has to say about how we should face the trials that come our way, even just a few verses after he instructs us to always trust in the Lord:

> My son, do not despise the LORD's
> discipline,
> and do not resent his rebuke,
> because the LORD disciplines those he
> loves,
> as a father the son he delights in.
>
> —PROVERBS 3:11–12

God isn't a helicopter parent. He doesn't make everything go your way and give you everything you want, because He knows that what you really need is to be mature and complete so that you are not lacking anything.

Consider trials from the perspective of Tim Keller's analogy of working out at the gym.[20] Let's say you begin doing biceps curls—not that I do, but let's imagine we are people who do biceps curls. You'll quickly notice that you feel like you're getting weaker with each curl. With every rep your arms feel more like noodles. But guess what? The weaker you feel you're getting, the stronger you're becoming. That's how strength training works. You use resistance to grow. If you learn endurance in trials, you initially feel like your faith, patience, and strength are getting weaker. You won't feel like you're getting stronger, but you are. With that in mind, consider Paul's words in 2 Corinthians 12:7–10: "Therefore, in order to keep me from becoming conceited, I was given a thorn in my flesh, a messenger of Satan, to torment me. Three times I pleaded with the Lord to take it away from me. But he said to me, 'My grace is sufficient for you, for my power is made perfect in weakness.' Therefore I will boast all the more gladly about my weaknesses, so that Christ's power may rest on me. That is why, for Christ's sake, I delight in weaknesses, in insults, in hardships, in persecutions, in difficulties. For when I am weak, then I am strong."

So what do you do when you feel your weakness—when even one more biceps curl of life feels like way too much? Here's what James has to say about it: "Let perseverance finish its work" (1:4). "Let" is an interesting word choice. It's passive. If I said, "Let it go," I'd mean, "Take your hands off, stop trying to control whatever is in your grasp." In other words, perseverance is not something we do, it's something we need to let God do to us as we give up trying to figure it all out on our own. This is what it means to submit to God in your trials. "All your ways," remember? Not just the ways in which you feel strong. In fact, any way in which you feel weak or incomplete also needs to be submitted to Him. There's good news at the end of James 1:4: when the work is finished, "you may be mature and complete, not lacking anything." Through this trial, you'll become equipped for more.

If we let them (that is to say, if we let God work in them), hardships and trials can strengthen character (Rom. 5:3–4). I'm sure you've heard the story of a butterfly banging its wings against the wall of its cocoon to break free from its incasement. If someone were to try to help it escape by making a hole in its cocoon, the butterfly wouldn't gain the necessary strength to survive on the other side.

When life goes smoothly, it's easier for me to rely on my own strength. It has been in the painful struggles that I've most passionately clung to Christ. John Calvin says, "The more we are afflicted with adversity, the surer we are made of our fellowship with Christ."[21] Nobody gets through life without facing some serious trials, and you know what this confirms for me? The fact that Jesus extends His kindness to all of us. Through our suffering, we are all given the opportunity to really know Him. Through our struggles and pain and trials of many kinds, Christ kindly removes the illusion of self-sufficiency and woos us deeper into intimate surrender.

Our task in suffering, therefore, is not just to endure it but to embrace the one who knows it perfectly and find intimate fellowship with Him and His body, the church, which we've needed all along. If the goal of my life is to know God and make God known, then knowing Him through struggle and pain is not optional. Our pain gives us a unique opportunity to know God more because we get to know His. We can start to understand why He endured it, why He thought it was worth it.

I'm not saying I do this right all the time, but my trials are increasing my awareness of other people's needs. Yesterday, I hosted a Bible study. A lady came who was on the verge of tears, one intentional question away from bursting forth with a full-on ugly cry. And then she did cry because someone cared enough to ask her questions. Honestly, I didn't have much compassion yesterday. I was in a hurry to get to where I was going. My friend was the one who asked questions. Today, as I sit here in the thick of thinking through one of my own trials, I'm becoming more aware of that woman.

Let perseverance finish its work so you don't lack anything. I can right now let my sadness do something in me to make me more equipped for next Monday's Bible study, more available to see the pain within someone else who is facing a trial. That's what submitting our trials to Him means—being open to the idea that they'll change us in a way that He will use for good.

IMPRESSIVE TO IMPACTFUL

The first message I gave after Randy died was to a camera.

I didn't know whether I would break down in front of an audience. The church I was speaking to conveniently invited me to speak to a room full of production techs who would be behind cameras, running slides for the message that would be filmed and then simulcast to the seven campuses that weekend.

I finished the message. It was on trials. I ended with an "amen" and suddenly became self-conscious. The lights faded to black, and I felt so empty. This was the moment I'd normally go backstage and call or text Randy.

And today, I couldn't.

For a few moments, the whole room was dark and silent. The cameras turned off and the lights turned back on, but I kept my eyes closed. When I finally opened them, I realized I had been holding my breath, too, and I exhaled. It hurt. I tried to breathe out the hopelessness and the confusion, but all I felt was pain. I needed the air, though, so I just kept breathing. It was all I could do. The lead pastor walked from the back of the room toward me. I didn't really want to hear anything he had to say. People can be insensitive to pain. I could barely lift my head. Once our eyes met, he said, "This is going to be a really different season for you."

Really? You think so? I said nothing.

"You're going to be moving from being really impressive to really impactful." He took his time with the next statement, eye contact steady. "Because pain is relatable."

Before Randy died, people who heard me speak may have been impressed with me, but that didn't mean they related to me. Now, because of my pain, I have a new common ground with people. My pain allows me to relate to the pain of others.

Pain allows us to relate to the pain of Christ Jesus. James experienced pain and used it to relate to others in his writing. He writes in that first verse to the brothers and sisters in the family of God, the Jewish followers of the Messiah, who are all suffering together. This type of perspective and potential in trials, in pain, is only possible for those who belong to Christ. Christianity does not promise freedom from pain. Instead, our faith empowers us to endure pain and know our Savior and our brothers and sisters through it. And this is the grace of God for the world. The fact that Christians are not exempt from suffering but are empowered to suffer differently is one of the most potent testimonies we have in this broken world.

Psychologist James Pennebaker did a long-term study on trauma survivors. Pennebaker wanted to understand the different reactions to trauma; some people face trauma and are devastated, while others become somehow more joyful than they were before the traumatic experience. Researchers thought there would be a correlation between the nature (sexual, physical, emotional) and size of the trauma and the recovery. Their hypothesis was wrong. The results found zero correlation between the nature and size of the trauma and the recovery. Instead, the number one commonality among people who grew after trauma—who became more joyful through it—was the presence of friends, family, or a support group to help them process their pain.

Trials are inevitable. Sharing your pain with others, though? Becoming relatable? That's a choice. It's the choice Jesus made, and it's the choice Scripture continually points us toward. "Therefore, since we are surrounded by such a great cloud of witnesses, let us throw off everything that hinders and the sin that so easily entangles. And let us run with perseverance the race marked out for us, fixing our eyes on Jesus, the pioneer and perfecter of faith. For the joy set before him he endured the cross, scorning its shame, and sat down at the right hand of the throne of God. Consider him who endured such opposition from sinners, so that you will not grow weary and lose heart" (Heb. 12:1–3).

These words from Hebrews spark something in me—they remind me that I'm not doing this alone. Isn't that what our trials do? They remove the illusion of our aloneness. We've all suffered. And in becoming one of us, Jesus endured more suffering than we can imagine. Jesus endured the cross for the joy set before Him, and that joy was us. It's hard to believe, but it's true. There was only one thing in heaven the Trinity didn't have before Jesus came to earth: us. In suffering through the thirty-three-year-long trial that was His life, Jesus was seeking relationship with us the only way a relationship would be possible. He endured the cross so He (and we) could have joy.

That pain you feel is an invitation—God wants to be with you. Taking on your trials by yourself, in your own power, is going back to autonomous living. You don't have to live that way. By enduring our trials with our eyes fixed on Jesus, we submit our trials to Him. He is with us through our trials, one painful step, one ragged breath at a time. Reach out to Him. He wants to be with you in the pain. God is not the stepdad from *The Sandlot*. He is there for the whole journey. And while He may not immediately take away the pain, He promises His presence.

Pain is relatable. We can relate to Jesus' pain, and by His grace, He uses our pain as a source of empathy for others. This journey is not solitary; it's a shared experience within a community of believers. Without trials we may convince ourselves we can find joy on our own. But if we let perseverance do its work, trials will lead us to the greatest joys imaginable: intimacy with Jesus and others.

Let's never suffer alone.

Asking Why

Why is this happening to me?

Has that thought ever crossed your mind?

Today, we're going to go to God with our frustration.

I invite you to make your trials personal with Him: "God, why is [blank] happening to me?"

How do you feel when you phrase it to Him that way? I want to invite you to sit with the question for a little while. Don't look away—look at Him. (If you wish, write your thoughts in the following space.)

Maybe nothing is coming to you right now, but know that He cares. He understands and knows what's happening to you. He sees you.

Take another breath. Even if you don't have an answer, you have Him.

CHAPTER 8

RISK

Trust in the LORD with all your heart
and lean not on your own understanding;
*in **all your ways** submit to him,*
and he will make your paths straight.

AS A SPECIES, humans kind of hate taking risks. I mean, c'mon—they're risky!

But what if I told you that risk is one of the best ways to step out of autonomy?

When you take a risk, you place yourself outside the zone where you can "figure it all out" on your own.

Risk is an overlooked part of living out our faith. John Wimber is famous for saying, "Faith is spelled R-I-S-K."[22] When you take risks, you will see God show up in surprising ways because you *need* Him to. I wonder if the reason we don't see God's power in our lives is because we play it too safe. I'm with Matt Chandler on this one: "Comfort is the god of our generation."

On our ten-year anniversary, Randy and I had a lot to celebrate, but unfortunately, we would not be celebrating it at a dinner table on the beach in Hawaii. It was 2020. So like everyone else, we dropped the original plan. We'd get some to-go food from one of our favorite restaurants and simply enjoy each other for the evening.

We took a drive to Santa Monica, California. I was thinking about a few simple ways I could make this date "outside the box" while working within the parameters. *What about a few risks?* I'd listened to a super-interesting TED Talk on risk earlier that week. So I decided I'd take at least one risk on our anniversary date. We reached Santa Monica, parked, and walked the Promenade. I tried on some Lululemon stretchy pants in a boutique—my first little risk. Those pants, while forgiving in their stretchiness, left little to the imagination. I took a deep breath and stepped out of the changing room. Randy raised his eyebrows and smiled (behind his mask, but I could still see it) while motioning a question, "Two?" As in, "Should we get you two pairs?" I didn't need two, but I sure was grateful for his response to me. He was reminding me that he loved me right where I was at, just as I was, not some future version of me in a smaller size. We didn't get two pairs of the same stretchy pants, but we walked out of the store hand in hand, and I was grateful for my guy who lived out what he said. He liked me for me. The celebration of our marriage had begun.

We were dressed nicely because we were celebrating ten years of togetherness. On our way back to our car, we walked past the Tesla dealership. I'd always wanted to test-drive one and figured today was uniquely special, so I motioned toward the dealership and we walked inside. We were quickly confused for a couple that could afford one (our anniversary getup surely had something to do with that) and were invited to take a test drive.

Salesperson: "Due to our current restrictions, you'd be

taking the test drive without any of our representatives going with you. It's difficult to maintain distance inside of the car."

Me: "So we'd take the car alone?"

Salesperson: "That's right."

Me: "Yes! Thank you!"

Randy (at the same time): "We'll see."

Randy worked a variety of jobs over his lifetime, mostly in the medical field or around the topic of safety. He even held the position of a "risk manager" for an ambulance company for a few years. His hesitancy was his training. As I was thinking, *Awesome! A Tesla for an hour!* Randy was thinking, *Is a joyride worth the risk of crashing a $90,000 car?* My husband and I made a good pair. I'm always up for the adventure, and he helped me thoughtfully consider the risk. Since his death, I risk less when it comes to safety but more when it comes to faith.

That night, risk won. We took the keys and off we drove down the Pacific Coast Highway for an hour, enjoying the features of a pricey car but, ultimately, celebrating our relationship. Obviously, we had him drive.

After the Tesla adventure, we got our food to go, drove forty-five minutes home in our Toyota, and discussed the topic of risk. I told my husband about the TED Talk I had heard: a guy lived for far too many years under the cloud of a moment of rejection he had experienced at the age of six. He wanted to take risks but always came back to that moment of childhood shame and decided against each opportunity to try something new. After googling "How do I overcome the fear of rejection?" he found www.rejectiontherapy.com. The site would send him prompts for the next thirty days that, if he followed through, would certainly lead to rejection—little risks like "request a burger refill." Through this brand of exposure therapy, and hopefully with some good laughs along the way, he'd learn how to live without fear of rejection because he'd face it daily and live to tell the tale. His thirty-day adventure turned into one hundred days, which turned into a remarkable number of speaking invitations to share the hilarious stories of asking to borrow one hundred dollars from a stranger or to be a "Starbucks greeter" for an hour.[23]

We got home and set our takeout on the table. I sat across from my husband of ten years and told him how much I loved the risks we'd taken in the past and that I wanted to risk more for my faith for the next thirty days as well. I wanted to take one risk for Jesus per day.

Taking this risk experiment was an invitation to live beyond my capacity because I found God there. God hangs out in places beyond our comfort zone, places that require His power. He is in the deep waters, so to speak. If all we ever do is splash around in the shallows, we'll never see the power of God at work. That, I'm convinced, is why so few people see God working in their lives. They genuinely don't need Him.

After we lost Randy, it became so clear to me that loving anybody in the first place is a tremendous risk—a risk worth taking. My risk experiment was years ago—December 2020. Randy died about two months later. I can see now how playing with risks and rejections prepared me for what would happen in the coming years. I kept taking small risks, even after the challenge was over. The small risks loosened my grip. Placing myself in situations, even silly ones, that were full of potential rejection showed me how much I valued control in my daily interactions. I wanted to hand that control back to God, to submit my time to Him. Through these small risks, Jesus was telling me, "Megan, you don't have to figure everything out on your own. You can trust Me, even when you don't know what's going to happen."

If you're looking for ways to loosen your own grip, a practical road map to stop "figuring it all out," I'd recommend some rejection, maybe even your own risk experiment.

Here's what my risk experiment looked like. Each day I tried to think about what Jesus would do if He were me. Whenever I felt the little nudge from the Holy Spirit to remember someone or do something, I would do my best to catch that moment (by the grace of God) and say yes to it. Honestly, going in I assumed that the nudges would be massive—share the gospel with a mean coworker or pay the mortgage for a family—but as it turned out, they were simple moments of opening my heart to what Jesus might do if He were me. And the truth is, He would do life differently than I naturally would do on my own.

He would prioritize time with our heavenly Father.

He would look people in the eyes.

He would smile and offer a word of encouragement.

He would relax.

He would applaud faith.

He would say yes to my five-year-old's invitation to ride scooters around the block. That was the first yes. The first risk.

DAY 1

"Mom, do you want to ride around the block with me?"

First a Tesla, then a scooter. Apparently, Jesus was all about the wheels.

I didn't have time in my schedule to play, but I risked it. We scootered around the neighborhood until we ran into his little buddies down the street who pulled out their scooters as well. I began a conversation with the mom of those kids and her sister. We shared some small talk, and the thought crossed my mind when asking a few questions to my mom friend's sister, *Be mindful of her circumstances*.

There are a lot of ways to be generous. Some are obvious: putting money in the offering basket or signing up for the GoFundMe. Sometimes we can be generous with our time, doing something helpful for someone else—providing a ride to the airport or listening when someone needs a space, an ear, and a heart to process with. One overlooked aspect of generosity, and also of faith lived out, happens in the mind. I've always appreciated my husband's ability to be thoughtful but never took the time to understand it until the day I felt prompted in my heart to think about the circumstances of my neighbor's sister.

Mindfulness is an act of love and generosity. Replacing your self-interest with thoughts of what it must be like for someone else is risky. But it's also loving. What pressures and desires was she experiencing in her late twenties? Likely the desire to be married, have her life together, have a good answer to the inevitable and overwhelming question, "What are you doing with your life?"

I thought, I wondered, and then I prayed. Quietly. And realized, in prayer, that prayer was the next step for her. Quite out of the blue, after a brief conversation on the beauty of pickleball, I asked if I could pray with her. This was a risk for sure. The potential for rejection was there. She needed intimacy with the Father, so I offered to lead her there. She responded to my question with a tentative "Uh, sure," and after a minute with our eyes closed and our minds opened to God's heart, I opened my eyes to notice tears streaming out of hers. She felt cared for. She felt cared for by her heavenly Father, and He'd used a small yes to a scooter invitation to get there.

Later that evening I asked if I could pray for some other neighbors. I was on a roll. I kept hearing the word "anxiety" come from my neighbor, and I knew Paul's invitation in Philippians 4:6 not to be anxious but to go to God, so I knew how to respond to his anxiety. I asked if I could pray. To my chagrin, their two-year-old began to dance during my well-intended prayer. I found myself frustrated while praying until

I took my own advice and decided to let my anxiety lead me to greater openness, and God opened my eyes to the freedom my neighbor longed for, the freedom of looking a lot more like a two-year-old dancing than a frustrated adult who had their own agendas and anxieties.

Day one was full of prayer. The risk God invited me to take on day one was realizing I couldn't help what was going on in someone else's soul, but there was someone who could. By prayer I presented requests to God and watched the peace of God keep out the bad thoughts and warm hearts with the good. The peace of God reminded my neighbor's sister that she didn't have to have life figured out to live well in the now. And the peace of God showed my other neighbor the freedom of faith found in a willingness to dance, forgetting about the silly pressures of the world that prevent us from enjoying it. On day one, risk and rejection and generosity all took place together.

Day 2

My dad searches for opportunities to encourage people.

Some people are generous with their money, others are generous with their thoughts, but my dad? He's generous with his words. I've heard him say "Meg, I'm so proud of you" at least once a month for the past five years. And the best part is that he doesn't say it only when I've performed well. He says it out of the blue. He builds me up toward excellence instead of simply clapping along with others who are waiting to be impressed before they clap.

We were hosting a youth training at our home, and forty volunteers packed our house to learn about mental health. I stood at the door saying my goodbyes when an encouraging thought crossed my mind as Daniel was walking by. Daniel wasn't like a lot of the other youth leaders and aspiring pastors

I've encountered. He could stand in front of a crowd, but he did well in one-on-one conversations too. What made him so good in those settings was that he was not afraid to show his emotions. So I pulled him aside and encouraged him for his sensitivity. While a lot of male youth leaders are applauded for their enthusiasm, not many are appreciated for their sensitivity.

"Well done, Daniel. You're following after the Man of Sorrows. Your sensitivity to others is meaningful. Keep it up."

Was that what He wanted me to say? I have no idea. But I risked it—I said what I thought Jesus wanted me to say. Daniel walked away stronger, not because emotions are weak but because he was looking like the Man of Sorrows when he embraced them.

DAY 7

In a culture that glorifies busyness and productivity, taking a weekly Sabbath is risky. Take Chick-fil-A, a notable example of this risk, choosing to close its doors on Sundays. Can you imagine losing a full day of income by being closed on Sundays when all your competitors are open for business? Dismissing the pressure to constantly achieve and earn and be productive is risky.

Taking a day of rest each week has become essential for my family. It helps us live better—more eye contact and heart time with my little boys and less time chasing accomplishments, which doesn't bring the satisfaction it promises. This is the heart of why God gave us the Sabbath. We have to risk that God is indeed the provider He promised He is. The Sabbath is a simple yet incredibly powerful tool God uses to train us to take our eyes off ourselves and our own sufficiency and autonomy and fix them on Him as the source of everything.

I think that's what Jesus did when He rested. He looked

people in the eyes. He laughed. And He made sure to thank His Father for everything He had made. Jesus worked hard—of course, He did. But He didn't waste time trying to "figure it all out."

In many ways, I remain a product of my culture: every single time my family rests, I have to resist the thought that we're "doing nothing" that day. We're doing something important: we're taking a risk. We're risking time and actions. We're trusting that God does have everything under control. All rest is an act of radical trust. It is our saying that we understand that the world does not go around by our efforts. And often, in resting, we limit our productivity in costly ways and are forced to trust that God will take care of us.

I've kept risking by continuing to rest on the Sabbath. And this risk never takes anything away from me, except maybe anxiety; it gives me space to recognize how great He is. Time to thank Him. Time to prepare for the next risks He's going to call me to.

Days 9–57

What I was surprised to find over weeks of saying yes to the Holy Spirit's nudges was that they were simpler than I expected. More often than not, they were small acts of love. Each nudge was bringing dignity to someone who could easily be overlooked.

It was talking to the serving staff at a dinner prepared for the speakers at a conference.

It was stopping to pray with people right at that moment instead of saying that I would later.

It was already watching when my son said "Mom, watch!" instead of glancing down at my phone.

It was choosing to talk with the lady in the corner when the famous Christian speaker was a handshake away.

It was wrestling with the Lord for strength and patience to listen to someone who needed to process their pain.

It was sending the text when God brought someone to mind.

It was getting up with the alarm to memorize a verse of Scripture when sleep felt more necessary.

When recounting the definition of love in 1 Corinthians 13, Paul reminds us that love is not necessarily inspirational or passionate, clever or persuasive, loud or showy. It's patient and kind. It is not self-seeking. It "keeps no record of wrongs" (v. 5). It's not easily angered. What surprised me most on this journey of risk was the truth that Paul concludes with: "Love never fails" (v. 8).

Throughout my risk experiment, I was waiting for the epic moments of failure. But the surprise was that risking for God became easier over time. Perhaps this was because God answered each risk like He answered the great faith risks in the Bible: with His presence. When Moses asked, "Who am I that I should go to Pharoah and bring the Israelites out of Egypt?" God answered, "I will be with you" (Ex. 3:11–12). I was anticipating some big failures, and to my surprise, I wasn't rejected once. Why? Because each risky moment was simply me offering love. To pray for someone. To encourage someone. To get to know a cashier. To look a homeless woman in the eyes and ask what she needed more than anything. To my surprise, her answer wasn't "I need money." The lady told me she needed a job.

While I don't know the end of the story for the lady without a home, I did make some calls. Our conversation started after I saw her digging through my trash for cans in my front yard. At first, I was uncomfortable. But within thirty minutes, we were hugging and crying in the rain. I knew that talking to her was my next Spirit-led risk. It felt like a strange Hallmark movie. I got on the phone with my sister who could set up a few job interviews. I described the woman as a hard worker, willing to do whatever it took to make ends meet.

You know, I feel a bit uncomfortable sharing stories where I'm a hero who does something right. The truth is the real hero is in me (yes, I'm talking about Jesus). He prompts me to do some pretty risky things. Mostly, I say no. Every once in a while, like in the Hallmark moment with the lady by the trash, I go with it.

Love didn't fail.

People didn't reject love.

I know that sometimes they do. I like how Jim McMahon put it: "Yes, risk-taking is inherently failure-prone. Otherwise, it would be called sure-thing-taking." But I'll tell you, risk is possible because the one we're risking for *is* a sure thing. The risk journey was just as much for me as it was for anyone I was stopping to notice or listen to or pray for.

I wonder if this is what Peter found when he walked on water. Maybe he found his greatest source of strength not while performing the miraculous but in the moment he was sinking and finally reached out his hand to take hold of Christ Himself.

God answers our inadequacy not with affirmation but with His presence. "I will be with you." That's why risk is so powerful and important. When we are out of our depth, we open ourselves (and others) to an encounter with the presence, power, and love of God. We don't look for His presence when we're comfortable. Could it be that constant comfort is a sign of autonomy, of believing the lie that we can do it ourselves? Yikes.

The risks I took during this challenge felt small and not necessarily even mentionable. But I believe that God cares about the small things we do for Him too—little risks are still risky. I wonder if that's what the kingdom of God is like, giving dignity to an unseen person, telling someone you believe in them, saying the nice thing you've been thinking about someone for years, stopping to pray in the moment instead of saying you'll pray in general.

What I discovered on this risk journey is that what I used to think was risk-taking is really Christlikeness, which makes a life of faith worth the risk. When I step outside of my own ability to control the outcome, I submit to the one who is already in control of it.

What do you have to lose?

Your autonomy?

Turns out, that's everything you've been hoping to lose all along.

GO TO GOD

Risky Possibilities

Maybe you've gotten this far into the book and you're thinking, *Okay, I understand that autonomy is bad, but how do I stop acting in my autonomy?*

Well, friend, risk is a good way to kick out autonomy.

If you're in a situation where you can't figure it all out on your own, maybe you'll be less tempted to try.

Right now, go to God. Close your eyes, take a breath, open your heart to Him, and ask, "What risk or two do You want me to take?"

What comes up in your mind? Don't get on your own case if you get distracted. If you get distracted when you're asking Him about risk, write down what steals your attention.

How can you take a risk in one of those areas?

Resolve to take one risk—big or small—that came up while you were talking about risk with God.

Thank Him, in advance, for the possibilities brought on by that risk, and then go for it!

CHAPTER 9

FRIENDSHIPS

*Trust in the LORD with all your heart
and lean not on your own understanding;
in **all your ways** submit to him,
and he will make your paths straight.*

A NEWER FRIEND walked into my house with a case of the grumps. She didn't try to hide it, and I was grateful.

Grateful? Yes! I was grateful because she finally let me see more of her. Up to that point, I had seen her only at her best. I had witnessed her enjoyment of adventure, her resilience amid plans going sideways, and the compelling kindness that she exuded. But this day, this grumpy Monday, she let me see more of her. She let me see her grouchiness, and guess what? I had the opportunity to love her more because I knew her more. This was the day we became real friends. I didn't just love the best version of her. I loved her as a friend, warts and all.

Warts? Yuck! Even the word is gross. Say it out loud: "Warts." See?! Bleh.

When I was in elementary school, I had a lot of warts all

over my knees. I frantically covered them with bandaids each morning before going off to school. I didn't discover until later that covering them with bandaids and not being consistent with changing the bandages out made the warts spread further, which meant adding even more bandaids, which meant even more spreading. The more I tried to cover them up, the more they spread. I anxiously tried to hide them from everyone because they're gross and I didn't want anyone to see them.

We do the same thing in friendships. We spend time and energy trying to cover the parts of ourselves we don't like, and in the process of managing everyone's perception of us, the stuff we don't like begins to grow and spread inwardly. Hiding parts of ourselves from our closest friends comes at the cost of feeling truly loved as we are. Hiding parts of ourselves takes so much of our time and energy, we don't have bandwidth to love imperfect people (ahem, ourselves and everyone else). It's easy to fall into the trap of not feeling loved completely because we don't show a full, complete version of ourselves. If we sense that the incomplete self we're offering is loved, we still don't feel truly loved. Trying to live out friendship halfway is not submitting our friendships to God. Through Scripture, He shows us the purpose of friendship and how to be a real friend—warts and all. Hiding parts of ourselves from our relationship with God comes at the cost of truly experiencing His love too.

WILL YOU BE MY FRIEND?

I expected friendships in adulthood to come easily like they did in childhood. I wonder when we grew out of asking that audacious question, "Do you *want* to be my friend?" Some people probably retired that question when they hit adolescence. Others never dared to ask it again after the first time someone responded no. What was it for you? Maybe it was the moment you picked up on someone else's signal and knew immediately, *Nah. They don't want to be friends with me.*

Once I hit my late twenties, after years of college and camp friendships, I thought incredible friendships would just happen. I had what Dietrich Bonhoeffer refers to as the "wish-dream" for friendships.[24] A wish-dream is an idealized and perhaps even unrealistic vision or fantasy for what you think something or someone should be like. My friendship wish-dream was a friend who would show up when I needed her, love the Lord with all her heart, parent her children (who happened to be the exact same age as my children) in the same way I did, listen to my struggles with compassion, be vulnerable about her struggles (but need only, like, fifteen minutes a week to get in all the relevant info), vacation with the same low-maintenance vibe I did, and be consistent in "just checking in."

I kept waiting for these friendships to happen.

I waited a long time.

By the time I hit my thirties, I was still waiting. The women whose paths I crossed were busy, or they seemed to have enough good friends already, or they were too shallow or too intense or too needy; to be honest, they were probably comparing me with their own wish-dreams. I now realize that we were all probably playing the "bandaid and warts" game, hiding our true selves from one another.

Most of us don't, as Proverbs 3:6 encourages us to, submit friendships to God's direction. Four years ago, I thought that everyone else had satisfying friendships and wondered how in the world I was missing out, but I didn't talk about it much. I didn't know how to make or maintain good friendships. I just had good moments with people from time to time. I assumed everyone else had that "good friendships" thing figured out. That was me. Is it you?

Having friendship wish-dreams is idolatry. Subconsciously,

we've believed we're entitled to good friends with little effort. From this place of entitlement, we balk at the idea of real friendship—of loving others with their imperfections and being loved with all our own warts too. Yikes. It's a scary prospect. No wonder we try to use wish-dream friendships to fill the gaps of insecurity within ourselves. Because that, at its core, is what idolatry is: using something or someone other than God to fill a need within ourselves that only God was intended to fill. When our idols fail us (when friendships aren't perfect), we then put distance between us and imperfect people.

What, you don't automatically perfectly love the imperfect people in your life?

Yeah, neither do I.

That's why we need Jesus. He knows we need real friendships, not wish-dreams, and by extending His perfect friendship to us, He gives us the strength for the real thing.

Understanding God's wisdom for friendship doesn't mean tossing out the idea of having good human friends; think about it, Jesus surrounded Himself with them. It just begins with finding wisdom in our friendship *with God*. Once we find true friendship with God, we're given not only the essential relationship we need but also a model for how to be a friend to others. God's desire for us is that we'll be who we really are in our friendships—our true selves, warts and all. In true friendship with Him, and submitted to His way of friendship with others, we can let go of that lonely struggle, that desire for our way instead of God's way (yep, autonomy again!). There is so much hope, friend, because a friendship with God defeats autonomy at its core.

Befriending Jesus

There's something you need to know. God wants to spend time with you. And I know that you want to spend time with Him too.

Then why don't you? God designed a relationship with you and even stopped all His work to prioritize it. Let's go back to the pinnacle of His creation: you. Did you know that the order of His creation pays you multiple compliments? Not only were you the pinnacle of creation, but day seven also speaks of what God does because of you. The Creator pauses His work and spends the day with humanity.

God created Sabbath as a model for us to follow, thus giving us an opportunity to trust Him to provide for us without our working all the days that we might. From the beginning, He was leading us away from autonomy and toward Him. He modeled resting so that we might submit our way of scheduling to His way, the practice of rest. Sabbath has always been less about a law and more about love. The first day of rest was full of spending time with those whom God loves. God did it with us on day seven. He stopped working to be present with us. God wants to love you. He even demonstrated His love for you in sending Jesus (Rom. 5:8). He wants you to find security in His love (Eph. 3:14–21). He desires for you to find everything you need in a relationship with Him. He wants what is best for you. He is fully available at all times. He pursues you when you least deserve it. He knows all of you and *still* loves you. Oh, what a friend we have in Jesus.

But just like any good friend, Jesus doesn't hold back the advice we really need to hear. About friendship, I believe He would say something like, "Once you discover the riches of our friendship, focus on being a friend instead of trying to find another perfect one." Because you won't find another one; Jesus is the only perfect friend.

This reminds me of the parable of the good Samaritan in Luke 10, specifically the question Jesus asks at the end. The man who asked a question that led Jesus to tell the parable in the first place asks Jesus, "Who is my neighbor?" (v. 29). In other words,

"Who deserves to have me love them as I love myself?" But at the end of the story, Jesus flips the script by saying, "Now, who was a neighbor to the man beaten by robbers?" (v. 36, paraphrased). In other words, "The question is not who deserves your neighborliness, but how far are you willing to go to be a neighbor to those in need?" Jesus changes the question. It's not "Who is my neighbor?" but "To whom will I be a neighbor?"

As you consider how to be a good friend, listen to Jesus' words: "Do to others as you would have them do to you" (Matt. 7:12; Luke 6:31). Jesus' words are so practical here. What do you wish someone would do for you? Do to someone else *as* you would have them do to you. There are fun ways to live this out. Do you wish someone would randomly drop off a coffee for you at work? Drive to Starbucks right now and pick up one for you and one for them. When you see a mom taking a picture of her husband and kiddos in front of the castle at Disneyland, offer to grab her iPhone so she can get in the pic. Come to think of it, I wish I was in so many amazing pictures that I have of my kiddos. Do you want someone to check in on you? Shoot a text to someone else. Do you wish someone would follow up with you about whatever you discussed last week? Try to remember what someone else talked about last week and follow up with them about it.

Paul echoes Jesus in Acts and says it's better to live this way. "The Lord Jesus himself said: 'It is more blessed to give than to receive'" (20:35). So far, I've brought up some of the easier ways to do this. There are also some challenging ones, like asking for forgiveness from the people who you wish would apologize to you. Remember Paul and Jesus' words: it's blessed to live in this way. When it comes to your friends, think of just one. What do you wish they would do to or for you? Jesus' advice is to go first!

The reason you can focus on being a friend instead of searching for friends is because, remember, you already have a perfect friend in Jesus. Listen to these words from John: "We love because he first loved us" (1 John 4:19). I wonder if Jesus' phrase "No one has greater love than this: that he lay down his life for his friends" (John 15:13 TLV) is less about sacrificing for your friends (although I think Jesus would urge us to do that too) and more about seeing that there is no greater friend than the one you already have access to: Him.

So let's talk about befriending Jesus. His friendship with you, like all friendships, is not one-sided. He wants you to reach back to Him in friendship, in the imperfect way that you're going to do it. That is a delight and desire of His heart. In John 15:15 Jesus says, "I no longer call you servants, because a servant does not know his master's business. Instead, I have called you friends."

I am really forgetful. Seriously. I need help to remember obvious things—I need alarms in my phone to remember to check in on friends and to remember to pray for people I've said I would pray for. I've created reminders to do what I know I want to do. For example, each time I floss my teeth, I pray for my friends. I stop at stop signs and try to remember that I can't show the fruit of the Spirit if I'm living a hurried life. (If people are in my car when I come to a complete and full stop, I look them in the eyes and usually just smile. They wonder about me.) I pray Romans 12 every time I get on an elevator to remind myself to ask God to prepare me for worship wherever I go. Reminders—I need them.

I've started using the "make coffee" button on my coffee machine as a reminder to befriend Jesus. Honestly, these past few years are the first in which I've had a consistent morning quiet time. My rationale: Mornings are first. God asks us to give Him the firstfruits. When we acknowledge Him in the first things, we are more likely to acknowledge Him in the rest. Believe the hype. His love will overflow into the others in your life if He's the first person you talked to that day.

Back to my coffee: First, I press the button, and I show up and start to pray "Lord, I offer myself to You" just like it says to do in Romans 12:1, that we would offer ourselves as living sacrifices to God so that every act is an act of worship. Second, I imagine an onion. I imagine peeling away layers of all my roles and responsibilities and identities and struggles and say, "Who I am is not primarily my roles: a widow, a mother, a teacher. I'm not primarily my worry. I'm not primarily outgoing. At the core of me, Lord, I am in You and You are in me." I do this to peel back everything so that I can find my core identity in Christ. I rest in that secure identity for a moment. I'm more than my titles and responsibilities and worries. In Christ is who I am at the core. Third, I let my mind wander because I know my mind will wander to something that has captured my heart, and that is what Jesus wants to talk about. Our conversation is spontaneous and free and even a little bit random, just like a conversation with a good friend. Finally, I listen to Him. There's a prompting every time: some work He's set before me, some sin that needs to be confessed, some person who needs a word of encouragement. He always directs me to love.

To summarize, these four steps are:

1. *Show up.* "Lord, I offer myself to You." Present yourself as an act of worship.
2. *Peel away.* Remember you're more than your titles and fears. You're in Him and He is in you.
3. *Let your mind wander.* Share it all. This is Jesus' cue to chat just like you would talk with a good friend.
4. *Listen and obey.* Listen and let Him guide you toward love.[25]

Once you realize your primary needs for security and love are met in Christ, and you start befriending Him yourself, you're going to see Him as both your model for friendship and your strength to live it out. Only Jesus does everything that Scripture asks of a friend.

Pause for a second. If that makes you think anything along the lines of *Well, then Jesus is the only friend I need*, let's sort that out right now. That state—Jesus being your only friend—is never what Jesus wanted. His perfect love compels us to reach out in love to others. This whole friendship-with-other-humans thing is not optional. His prayer in John 17 shows that His love moves from us and Him to us and Him and everyone else. This is why we have a church and why it's important to be a part of it. It's not just you and Jesus, and it was never supposed to be.

That said, our other friends won't be like Him (and you won't be like Him for anybody else!). So how do we live out His perfect love in our imperfect friendships? The oft-quoted J. C. Ryle tells us that "friendship halves our sorrows and doubles our joys."[26] The Word of God concurs; friendship is meant for both joy and sorrow, laughter and trouble. Proverbs offers this wisdom on friendship: "A friend loves at all times, and a brother is born for a time of adversity" (17:17). A friend loves at all times, which includes the good times, the bad times, the embarrassing times, the shameful times, the funny times, the when-they're-mean times, and the depressed times. If we spend our energy trying to cover up the negative, offering and showing others our best in the hope of being loved at our best, friendships become yet another place to hide from God and from ourselves. If hiding and covering is what we bring to the table in our friendships, others will feel like they have to hide and cover too.

During the time this proverb was written, there would've been cultural obligations for family members to take care of one another. That is why "a brother is born for adversity." In other words, family members have a duty to take care of you in times of need. But what makes friendships great is that a friend's love for you is expressed at all times, not only in times of adversity, because a friend is someone who has chosen to love you, whereas a relative is obligated to love you.

"At all times" means you're available not only when it's convenient. Most people know you and want to know you because you're useful to them. Before you get all bent out of shape about that, I want you to realize that the people you have become friends with are useful to you in some way. Some of them are useful for having a good time. Some are useful for meaningful conversations. Some of them are useful for getting things done. When your life is falling apart, you'll notice different categories start to emerge. Some friends will say, "Call me if you need anything." Others will just show up. A brother "born for adversity" says, "I will do whatever it takes to keep you from falling into ruin. I'll be there even when it costs me something." I'd be willing to bet that those who just show up are drawing their strength to love you from their friendships with Christ.

Of course, not all friendships have the same purpose. I was told a long time ago that my friendships should fall into one of these categories: Paul, Barnabas, and Timothy. A friend who is a Paul is a mentor and guide, someone whose wisdom I can trust—typically, someone who has more life experience than I do. Did you know that you can be friends with people who are *decades* older than you? I dare you to try it. A Barnabas friend is a true partner. Remember when Barnabas testified before the apostles that Paul had changed? Talk about a friend in adversity. A Barnabas is someone with whom you can live the spiritual life, someone who is maybe even struggling with some of the things that you are. And anyone who is a Timothy is a person you're pouring into; the love of Christ is meant to be shared, and we need to seek out Timothys who need encouragement and experience. The real secret of those relationships is that you'll be even more blessed than the Timothy in question. "It is more blessed to give than to receive" (Acts 20:35).

Incidentally, friendship with Jesus and friendship with other Christians are not two different things. Remember, the church is referred to throughout the New Testament as the "body of Christ." This means that loving sisters and brothers in the church *is* loving Jesus. Jesus makes this connection clear in John 17. In Matthew 10:42, Jesus promises reward to any disciple who gives a cup of cold water "to one of these little ones." Jesus clearly has deep concern that we treat His body like, well, *His!*

At the Same Table

The year before Randy went to heaven, he told me he wanted to be ninety years old eating at the same restaurant in the same corner booth with the same guys being served by the same waitress for decades.[27] I stole his idea. I began to ask God to bring people to mind—women who would desire to go deeper with Jesus as we went deeper with one another. I didn't want a group of people to just catch up on life with; I needed people who would all be willing to stop hiding and covering and to open their lives before one another so that we might find Jesus together. My prerequisite for the gals I ended up inviting into this relationship was that they already had a deep, consistent, all-in friendship with Jesus. What ended up happening at that table put flesh on the idea that individual friendships with Jesus will overflow into our friendships with others. He makes real friendship possible.

First, God brought to mind Brooke. I thought, *Wouldn't it be amazing to hang out with Brooke consistently? She is the most thoughtful woman I've ever met.* I followed that thought with *She'll never say yes. She already has plenty of other friends who don't live forty-five minutes away.* I honestly thought it would be too good to be true if she said yes. I kept coming up with all sorts of excuses why she might say no. This, by the way, is why we rarely make invitations in the first place. It's easy to become convinced that people would rather not.

Then God brought to mind Alyson, a marriage and family therapist / spiritual director. She was an obvious win for the whole table. Then Susie, who is passionate about race, justice, and Jesus. During our first coffee date, I think I offended her on numerous occasions, but she didn't hold it against me. She told me how my words could be received as offensive but stayed in the conversation and kept talking and listening. She kept asking questions and let me be honest in my lack of understanding about how to hold racial reconciliation conversations. "An honest answer is a sign of true friendship," Proverbs 24:26 says (GNT). You don't want people around you who are fake, but you also don't want a friend who tries to hurt your feelings. Honesty needs to be gentle and drenched in love to be effective. I have felt loved by Susie's honesty.

Susie reminded me that we should invite Tiana, a powerhouse Black woman who passionately loves Jesus and knows Him deeply, even through pain. When everything went down with George Floyd, I came to the conversation shocked. Her response was, "You're shocked by all this, and I'm tired." Tiana continues to teach me the power and importance of sharing the whole truth, and nothing but the truth, so help me, God.

Then I asked God to bring one more. I waited and heard nothing but then not so surprisingly had a timely lunch date with Erin. Erin came out of a more legalistic church environment, has an incredible family, knows the truth, prays like a warrior, and is constantly in awe of the freedom we have in Christ by His Spirit. And then God brought Brit, our charismatic redhead who oftentimes claims dreams and visions as promises from God. I lovingly try to correct her theologically, and then they all come true. Gosh, it's almost frustrating how vibrant her faith is because of her confidence in discerning the voice of God. Yet she's humble. She's open to being wrong. Humble friends are my favorite kind of friends because I know they'll always be growing.

I found my table: Brooke, Alyson, Susie, Tiana, Erin, and Brit. We call ourselves "Deeper with Jesus," a name I got from Yvonne, the Paul in my life. We started meeting in December of 2019. Did you catch that? Remember what happened that next year? Yeah, I don't have to remind you of everything that transpired in AD 2020. The gift of our group was that we were divided over some topics but unified in Christ.

During all of 2020, I couldn't say the phrase "How could someone vote that way?" because someone at my table did vote that way. I couldn't say "How could you think *that*?" about anything because I knew someone who did think that. We were diverse and unified. The goal of our time together was to go deeper with Jesus as we went deeper with one another. That's friendship. It's not perfect. It's not hiding sin. It's not hiding beliefs. It's not hiding opinions. It's loving, which, by the way, is key to being a part of the body of Christ. And sometimes, loving someone has to come at the expense of trying to be right all the time. First Corinthians 12 talks about us all being a part of the body, and the next chapter starts by saying that, if we do something "but do not have love, [we are] only a resounding gong or a clanging cymbal" (1 Cor. 13:1). And doesn't social media sound a lot like a resounding gong or clanging cymbal? *Crash, crash, crash.*

The posts or comments we read online imply, "You should believe this . . ." *Crash, crash, crash.* "How could you . . ." *Gooong!* Social media is a lot of noise, which is why we have to be careful in our technologically connected world to find friendships and connect with friends by showing up face to face with them. We are too quick to call our social-media community our "friends" as we celebrate (internally) how many thousands of friends we have (which sociologists believe is a relational impossibility). Now contrast that with true friendship.

"A friend loves at all times." All times includes all times: when we're right, when we're wrong, when we're opinionated, when we're quiet, when we're loud, when we're sinful, when we're commenting on social media, when we're rude, and even when we're not physically present with one another. I will never forget Brooke, one of my (now) dearest friends, kindly and lovingly letting me know that I'm an amazing friend in the moment but pretty crummy at being consistent when we're not face to face. Ouch. She was right. I was good in the moment but not "at all times." I have a lot left to learn, and these gracious women are still walking with me; we're still going deeper with Jesus. But let me tell you something, it has never stopped being a sacrifice. Just getting to the table every other week is a sacrifice. Every time I think of something more "productive" I could be doing than investing in these friendships. But then I remember how the Deeper with Jesus group is realizing Randy's dream of real, deep relationships.

A dream of friendship that is submitted to God's ways takes time and patience and sacrifice from everyone involved. The good news is, He has already made the greatest sacrifice to call us His friends.

GO TO GOD

Time with Jesus

Maybe it's not the beginning of the day, but I want to go through part of my coffee routine with you. Let's go to Him together. Let's spend time with your perfect friend, the one who loves you the most.

1. Show Up

As I press the button to make my coffee, I say, "Lord, I offer myself to You."

This is a good thing to say at any time of the day. Let's do it now: "Lord, I offer myself to You."

"Therefore, I urge you, brothers and sisters, in view of God's mercy, to offer your bodies as a living sacrifice, holy and pleasing to God—this is your true and proper worship. Do not conform to the pattern of this world, but be transformed by the renewing of your mind. Then you will be able to test and approve what God's will is—his good, pleasing and perfect will" (Rom. 12:1–2).

2. Peel Away

Remember, you're more than your titles. List some of your roles here: Who are you? What do you do? Who are you for others? What are you feeling? List them, one by one.

Now place your finger on each of these roles or responsibilities as you say to Him, "I am not primarily this or that at the core, I'm in You and You are in me. I am [insert any word defining who you are in Christ, such as *chosen, accepted, beloved*]. Because *You are.*"

3. Let Your Mind Wander

Let your mind wander and share it all with your friend Jesus.

4. Listen and Obey

Last, as we wrap up the friendship chapter, ask God to bring to mind one friend. Ask God what He might have you say, know, or do in love. Let Him give you an idea and then say yes.

CHAPTER 10

MONEY

Trust in the LORD with all your heart
and lean not on your own understanding;
in all your ways submit to him,
and he will make your paths straight.

WHAT WERE THE last ten things you spent money on?

I'm serious. Pull out your phone, log in to your bank account, and check. How would you feel if we were sitting across a table from each other and I asked you to read your list out loud? What does your list reveal about the priorities of your heart?

If you want to know what's in your heart, follow the money. Your bank account reveals a lot about your heart. If you're thinking, *Wow, that's personal, Megan,* I'll level with you: that's exactly what I'm getting at. Money is personal. Talking about money is vulnerable. Because money, and the way we choose to use it, reveals something deep about our hearts.

That's why Jesus spent so much time talking about it. From the many parables where Jesus either mentioned or spoke directly about money, to the warnings to the wealthy in Luke 6, to the famous story of the rich young ruler, Jesus spent a good chunk of His ministry helping people think about their relationship with money. And in this—as in everything else—Jesus was being thoroughly biblical. It seems like He was preaching right out of the book of Proverbs.

RICH MAN, POOR MAN

The topic of money comes up frequently in Proverbs. Most of Proverbs was written by Solomon, who was out-of-this-world rich. And Jesus, well, for a person who didn't have much money, He talked about it a lot. But here's the funny thing. Jesus' teachings and Solomon's collection of proverbs both say the same thing about money: it should be a servant, not a master. And when money becomes your master, it's disastrous. The author of Proverbs 30 (who wasn't Solomon) wrote:

> Two things I ask of you, LORD;
>   do not refuse me before I die:
> Keep falsehood and lies far from me;
>   give me neither poverty nor riches,
>   but give me only my daily bread.
> Otherwise, I may have too much and
>   disown you
>   and say, "Who is the LORD?"
> Or I may become poor and steal,
>   and so dishonor the name of
>   my God.
>
> —PROVERBS 30:7–9

Does "my daily bread" sound familiar? That's what Jesus taught His followers to pray for. He didn't teach them to pray for more money. He didn't even teach them to pray for enough money. He taught them to ask their heavenly Father for what they needed *that* day. Jesus understood that both extremes—too much money or too little of it—create temptation. Like Proverbs 15:27 says, "The greedy bring ruin to their households, but the one who hates bribes will live." Have you ever played through an entire game of Monopoly with your family? Talk about "ruin to their households." Anxiety about money brings out the worst in all of us, even when it's fake money.

When Jesus preached about money, the crowd following Him probably felt nervous. But Jesus wasn't wringing His hands. He wasn't wondering about the future. He wasn't even asking for money when he talked about it; Jesus never asked His followers for money, not even once. Near the middle of His Sermon on the Mount (Matthew 5–7), Jesus brought focus to the way that we interact with our possessions. In respect to treasures—like money—Jesus tells us:

> Do not store up for yourselves treasures on earth, where moths and vermin destroy, and where thieves break in and steal. But store up for yourselves treasures in heaven, where moths and vermin do not destroy, and where thieves do not break in and steal. For where your treasure is, there your heart will be also. . . .
>
> If then the light within you is darkness, how great is that darkness!
>
> No one can serve two masters. Either you will hate the one and love the other, or you will be devoted to the one and despise the other. You cannot serve both God and money.
>
> —Matthew 6:19–21, 23–24

Jesus took a moment to point out how concerned His audience was about their stuff. Back in what I grew up calling "the

Bible days," people owned three things that were valuable: grain, precious metals, and cloth. Sound familiar? Pricey food, stuff made out of metal, and expensive clothing? Some things change; some things don't. But back then, they didn't have safe-deposit boxes. Instead, they had huge warehouses where they would store their wealth. The problem with the warehouses was that bugs and rats and thieves could get in and destroy or take everything. If someone was wealthy enough to have a warehouse, they spent a good chunk of time (and money) safeguarding it. The systems look different now, but we still spend a lot of time fretting about the stuff we've stored away.

But what Jesus was saying to these people (and to us) is this: "Have you noticed how worried you are about your stuff? The more stuff you have, the more worry you'll have. No matter how you store it, it could be taken away from you. Thieves could steal it. Moths and vermin could eat it. But no one can take away the treasure you keep in heaven."

He was telling the people to stop focusing on what they might gain on earth and start looking toward His kingdom. Did you hear that? We can use our money to partner with Jesus in building His kingdom! Or we can use it to build our own. We choose whether we invest in finite ways or in infinite ways. Money spent reveals the depth and location of our devotion. Remember what your list of ten showed you. What holds the attention of your heart—investments, charitable contributions, ice cream on Sunday afternoons? Are those things finite or eternal? It's not just about *what* you spend your money on, it's also about understanding the reasons why.

Look closely at the way you're using your money. Wherever your treasure happens to be, your heart is right there with it. That's why Jesus cares so much about this and talked so much about money. He doesn't want to obsessively monitor your spending habits. He just knows that your treasure and your heart are intertwined. You place value on whatever it is you're willing to spend money on, and He's keenly interested in what you value. Why? Because He values you, and He's after your heart. He didn't ask His followers for money, but He did ask, over and over again, for their hearts. He's asking you for the same thing. He deeply and passionately wants your heart, so He's, of course, going to discuss your finances.

TREASURE

Where your thoughts are is where your heart is, and recently, it has come to my attention that I think about money all the time.

I needed to do some soul searching about this, because this wasn't how I got started in ministry, and "worried about money" is not how I'm going to spend the rest of my life. Have you ever felt the freedom of working for practically nothing? Years ago, I spent six summers working at a Christian camp. The demands on the staff were reasonable considering how epic the environment was (and still is). But we made some less than responsible choices—we overworked, and we stayed up way too late. Once, just for fun, we calculated that we were working fourteen-hour days for $1.31 per hour. But it was so worth it to us. Around this same time, I started taking speaking engagements for $0.00 per hour. One of the first was at an all-nighter; I had the 2:30 a.m. time slot. Perfect. At a different event, my great reward for my time and my thoughts was a Chick-fil-A coupon for a single chicken sandwich. I would have to pay for the fries! It turned out that the coupon was expired, so I paid for the sandwich too. The point is, I didn't think about money all the time. I wasn't working for money, and I wasn't speaking for the sake of it. If any treasure was gained, it couldn't be stored on earth.

Then I started doing more and more speaking. Most of the time, the reward I received was a "Thank you, Megan!" or a gas card. I remember receiving my first honorarium. This was in 2008. After I gave an address at my alma mater, someone handed me an envelope and said, "Here's your honorarium." I didn't even know what that word meant. I opened the envelope and found a check for fifty dollars. *Wait a minute*, I thought, *I can get paid money for this?*

The worry didn't take hold right away, though. Just after Randy and I got married, we sat down to do our taxes together. He was doing a lot of it because he was good with money. After he ran our numbers for 2011, he called me over and said, "I'm okay with this, but just so you know, you are losing money doing ministry every year. You are working as a waitress to pay for your work in ministry." We both laughed when he reminded me, "Megan, this kind of thing is what I love about you."

Then, over time, the money started to matter to me. I started making decisions based on it. I started saying yes or no because of it. I started worrying about it. I started thinking about it a lot.

Do you think about money a lot too?

Can you remember when you first started thinking about it so much?

I was on a walk about a year ago, and I'm going to say that I was on a walk with God, because He's the one I was talking to, and we were talking about money. I was asking Him why it was so hard to trust Him with money. After all, I tell Him I trust Him consistently with my future, my pain, and my two young boys, and they are way more important to me than money. And the place we came to was this: I believe that God will take care of my kids and their future because I believe they are gifts from God.

But money? That's something I earned. That's mine.

While Psalm 24:1 sounded nice theologically ("The earth is the LORD's, and everything in it"), I don't think I practically believed money was His.

I came to a place in prayer on that walk where the Spirit

enabled me to become conscious of my worried conscience. "Lord, search me." I waited in expectation for God to reveal why my heart felt worried. My mind wandered to money as it normally did. Money and worry often show up together, and not just for me. In the Sermon on the Mount, Jesus reaches the climax in His discussion about money in Matthew 6:25 when He tells us not to worry. He first says "You cannot serve both God and money" (v. 24) and follows it up with "Therefore I tell you, do not worry about your life" (v. 25). I was concerned about money, and I was worried. Jesus knew exactly where I was coming from, and He patiently worked through it with me.

Rather than trying to pray away the worried thoughts about money, I tried another approach with God. I clasped my hands together as if cupping a ball. What, you don't pray with hand gestures? Consider this your invitation to try it. Back to my walk. My hands were cupped together, and I imagined my finances right there inside my palms. I noticed how tightly my hands were clenched. I hadn't done that on purpose. Then I realized the Holy Spirit already understood everything about my finances, knew my heart about money, and wanted to transform me as I looked at it with Him. I couldn't stay worried looking at it with the one who is not worried about a thing. My hands were in front of me, open and relaxed. Rather than seeing the worry about money as a problem to be solved, I saw it as a warning light on the dashboard of my soul to be addressed.

I yielded my worried conscience in a slow dialogue with the Holy Spirit. I invited Him to make me aware of the root of my worry. The Holy Spirit brought to mind what my soul needed to address, and He used my worry to locate where I hadn't yet submitted my ways to Him when it came to money. Because I thought money was earned and belonged to me, I felt all the pressure to make it. But when I opened it up and invited the Holy Spirit's perspective on it, I considered the same truth I already believed: "The earth is the LORD's, and *everything* in it" (Ps. 24:1, emphasis added).

I thought, *Money is the Lord's, and the talents I bring to a job are the Lord's. Opportunities I might have in the future are the Lord's. It's all His.* As His Spirit reminded me of the truth I already knew, I declared, "I'm going to trust You with this, God. And I'm going to trust You with my worry about it too. And I ask You to help me trust You with it because even though I'm telling You, 'I'm going to trust You,' I know that I won't, and I want Your help then too. I don't want to do any part of this on my own." And, friends, I felt freedom, the kind of freedom I hadn't felt in a long time, the kind of freedom I felt when I was running around working at that Christian camp for $1.31 per hour, knowing that it was all for God anyway. The freedom didn't come when the money poured in; the freedom came when I became aware that I wasn't carrying my financial burden alone. I felt like I was standing next to the wealthiest man in a room full of shoo-in investment opportunities. It felt like He said to me, "I'll pay for everything. Don't worry about it anymore." His Spirit is God's investment into me, to become everything He intends me to be, beginning that process exactly where I am.

He relaxed my heart as I vocalized my desire to trust Him more with everything in my hands.

I've had to make tangible adjustments in how I go about choosing ministry opportunities to live into what I desire: I don't want my ministry to revolve around money. What my sister (who manages logistics) and I decided was that she would be the only person to see the financial portion of a speaking request until I decided whether I would take it. These days, when it comes to honorariums, I always agree to the speaking event before I know what the honorarium is. I ask God if this is the best yes and we mutually move forward, even if there is nothing in it but an expired Chick-fil-A coupon.

Let's get back to Jesus' Sermon on the Mount. In Matthew 6:22, Jesus seems to stray from the money topic, saying, "The eye is the lamp of the body." He goes on, reminding His followers that if they are healthy, their whole bodies will be full of light. But self-deception is a real thing: "If then the light within you is darkness, how great is that darkness!" (v. 23). He's *still* talking about money. Jesus knows that some people think they can be secure both in God and in their money. It's not an uncommon thought, but it's tantamount to thinking that light and darkness give the same level of visibility. He knows that they've been duped.

We can't have two masters. Remember, money is either a master or a servant. And the darkness of divided devotion is not a devotion to both; it's a devotion to money, every single time. Money is going to be either a master or a servant in your life. God does not share the title. Is money your master? Let me ask you that another way: Does money dictate your decisions? Do you feel an overbearing weight of responsibility?

Or is money your servant?

When money is the servant, we seek God's kingdom with it. It serves the purposes God has laid on our hearts. Money becomes a tool instead of a taskmaster. When money is a servant, we are stewards. Second to sharing our faith, sharing our money may be the greatest tangible expression of our faith. Plus, there's a pretty sweet by-product: generosity lowers our anxiety because it simultaneously builds our faith.

Before we do anything else with our money, we should think about how to submit it to God and use it to love others. Then we can take care of our savings, taxes, debts, and spending. If you prioritize giving, dividing up the rest of the treasure will be done from a posture of contentment. And let me tell you, the feeling of contentment sure lasts longer than overspending.

Jesus is clear about this: "Do not store up for yourselves treasures on earth" (Matt. 6:19). Not only can those treasures be destroyed, but the need for treasure will destroy you. Jesus sought the other kind of treasure, the kind of treasure that He came to earth to seek in the first place. Paul gives a new dimension to Jesus' treasure when he prays in the first chapter of his letter to the Ephesians "that the eyes of your heart may be enlightened in order that you may know the hope to which he has called you, the riches of his glorious inheritance in his holy people, and his incomparably great power for us who believe" (vv. 18–19).

Did you catch that phrase "eyes of your heart"? I'll take the liberty of reminding you what Jesus says about eyes: "The eye is the lamp of the body. If your eyes are healthy, your whole body will be full of light" (Matt. 6:22). Paul is praying that the Christians in the Ephesian church will understand who they are. Paul prays that by knowing who they are, they'll know not only where treasure belongs but also what treasure is. To drive the point home, Paul makes it clear that the people of the kingdom are Jesus' "glorious inheritance" (Eph. 1:18).

Let's tie that all together: Jesus didn't try to gain money, but He did want heavenly treasure. He wanted treasure that nothing could destroy. He went so far as to make certain of it. He gave His own life to safeguard it: to safeguard "*you*, the riches of his glorious inheritance" (emphasis added). When Jesus surveyed the crowds gathered below to hear His Sermon on the Mount, He saw His great inheritance. He saw a thousand hearts He wanted to hold forever. With tenderness and compassion, He told His own treasures, "For where your treasure is, there your heart will be also" (Matt. 6:21). Jesus knew where His heart was. When Jesus preached about eternal treasure in heaven, He was thinking about *you*.

The treasure Jesus wanted is your heart.

INDEBTED

We are Christ's inheritance.

This perspective illuminates how we're supposed to interact with everything else. We're not in an even exchange with Him (i.e., we give Him something, He gives us something else). No! We *belong* to Him. We're His inheritance. "The earth is the LORD's, and everything in it" (Ps. 24:1). It's all His. We're His. This is the root of our freedom in Christ. Anything we "have" belongs to the one who gave up His life for us. This frees us up in the autonomy department; not only can we not do anything on our own, but we belong to God, just like everything we "own." We can give it freely. We, who have been forgiven of so much, should hold our money with open hands. How do we do this? Luke 7:36–50 holds up an imperfect woman as the perfect example. I'll paraphrase.

Jesus and His disciples are invited to a BFPP: big, fancy Pharisee party. Everyone's dressed in their best, and everyone is on their best behavior. You can practically smell the money spent. Everyone sits down, with Jesus at the head of the table, and then *she* shows up. Luke distinguishes her as a woman "who lived a sinful life" (v. 37). She doesn't even knock. She pushes her way through to Jesus, crying the whole time. She bends down, washes His feet with her tears, and pours an entire jar of perfume—talk about smelling the money—over Him. And the Pharisees just sit there, mouths open. She wasn't invited; she is way beneath their social strata, and because of certain "reasons," none of them would want to be seen with her.

"If Jesus is a prophet," the host says under his breath, "wouldn't He know who's touching Him?" (v. 39, paraphrased).

Jesus replies out loud for the whole table to hear: "Two people owed money to a certain moneylender. One owed him five hundred denarii, and the other fifty. Neither of them had the money to pay him back, so he forgave the debts of both. Now which of them will love him more?" (vv. 41–42).

The Pharisee acquiesces, "I suppose the one who had the bigger debt forgiven" (v. 43).

The Pharisees keep their seats. The sinful woman is draped over Jesus' feet. He forgives her sins, but the Pharisees—they just get a nice dinner. Do you see the difference? Are you living like you've been forgiven of much?

Live indebted. Practice generosity. Let it all spill over. You've been forgiven. You can give freely. You won't do it perfectly every time, but you can start from a place of total indebtedness to Him. And sometimes, there will be other people to help you grow closer to God in this way. I know because I've met many, and I pray that they cross your path too.

The hospitality of Life Center church in Spokane, Washington, is unmatched. Each normal part of the "hiring a speaker" process was done with excellence. I arrived at the airport and, of course, there was someone holding a sign with my name on it. That made me smile because it reminded me of how I used to pick up friends from the airport. I would stand at the bottom of the escalator in baggage claim with a printout sign that said "T. Swift" or "Amy Grant" or "Adele." You should've seen my friends' faces as I started to wave frantically, drawing far too much attention to them.

When I got to the hotel there was a note thanking me for speaking to the students at the conference. It's normal to get one of these notes from a church or conference center. This church's note included, "Thanks for speaking to these students, who we happen to really love. We love these students and are so blown away that we'll get to love them through you." It was a beautiful reminder of what I do as a speaker: love people, not impress them. But the Life Center staff had left a second note in a second envelope. This is what it said:

A One-Hundred-Dollar Experience

The best gifts are experiences. Unfortunately, we can't send you to Hawaii with a bungee jumping voucher or have your childhood celebrity crush call you, but we can do something small. If someone unexpectedly gave you a $100 bill, that would feel pretty cool, right? So here's your chance to make someone feel pretty cool. Here is $100 to give away. Use it to bless someone however you see fit. We hope it's a great experience for you.

This church doubled down on the slogan "It's better to give than to receive." I had been given the gift of being able to be generous. This was a significant moment for me. Ever since Randy died, I've been on the receiving end of other people's generosity. I've had anonymous people pay for my kids' schooling and received checks in the mail from names I didn't recognize, although I could relate to the memo "hope from a fellow widow."

This church not only wanted me to love their students but also wanted to love me and my family by letting us join in on the extravagant, generous fun. They gave me a chance to be like Christ. I wanted to know precisely who God wanted me to give the hundred dollars to. I asked for it to be obvious. It wasn't obvious until a full two weeks after the conference. The one hundred dollars remained in my backpack, untouched for weeks.

One afternoon, my toddler fell and hit his forehead on a table. My father-in-law and I took him to the ER to see if he needed stitches, even though I knew he wasn't hurt too seriously. As we waited, I walked over to CVS to grab a five-dollar bottle of hydrogen peroxide for the wound. In the checkout line, I noticed that the woman at the front was price-checking each item in her filled-to-the-brim shopping cart. She was having to make difficult decisions to see what combination of needs and wants she could afford. The $3.26 four-pack of toilet paper was moved to the yes column, while the $0.59 mystery gel was placed back in the cart. The medicine was too expensive, the soap was okay because it was a cheap brand. I watched this unfold until God made the one-hundred-dollar-challenge obvious. *She's the one.*

I walked up to her and said, "Excuse me, you can stop price-checking because I'd like to buy everything for you."

Her eyes widened, and she asked, "What?"

I said to the cashier, "Yes, I'd like to buy all of it, plus this," and I handed him my $5 bottle of hydrogen peroxide.

"Are you sure?" the woman asked. I was more than sure. She stood frozen in shock until she remembered, "I have coupons, lots of coupons, for . . ."

"You won't need your coupons," I informed her. "I know God, and He's been unbelievably generous with me. He's real and really wants you to know Him too—"

"But wait, I have coupons," she interrupted.

"You can put away all of your coupons. God has been so generous with me, and I'm telling you, it's all covered. All of it. May God continue to bless you and show Himself to you." My card was already in the reader.

It *is* better to give than to receive. This experience was better than theme-park tickets or anything I've purchased online for myself to feel better for a moment. I got to experience a taste of what it must feel like for God to give away His grace. In covering the cost of everything I owe, He gives us everything we need in Himself. And I know this more because of the hospitality of a church, and because I prayed a specific prayer: "God, make it obvious." He will. He wants to show Himself through you.

"Your total comes to $105," the cashier said. No one would ever know but me and, well, everyone who reads this book, but the $105 minus my $5 peroxide equaled exactly the $100 I'd received in the envelope two weeks prior. Of course it did. God is in the details. We'll see it if we submit everything, including our money, to His purposes.

God provided all the essentials for a lady at CVS plus a little extra, and He provided it through me. Well, actually, through the church through me. And isn't that how it goes? God gave Himself for the church, and the church equips us to help others see what God is like. He's finding uses for earthly treasure for the sake of His inheritance, and He's the one responsible for the bottom line. And us?

We can put away the coupons.

We can relax.

He's going to cover everything.

GO TO GOD

Clasped Hands

Clasp your hands together as if cupping a ball and imagine your finances right there inside your palms.

Crack open a space in your hands, imagining the Holy Spirit swarming inside, searching your entire heart on money.

The Holy Spirit already knows your heart toward money but is searching it with you to transform your heart as you look at it.

Close your eyes and search your heart with the one who dwells there.

Slowly open your hands as you open your heart to God's ways regarding your finances.

Ask God for faith to trust Him.

Remember that He doesn't need your coupons or money.

Is there a particular way God might be inviting you to use your money this week to love someone? Write what comes to mind.

Remember this: He wants your heart.

CHAPTER 11

MISTAKES

Trust in the LORD with all your heart
and lean not on your own understanding;
*in **all your ways** submit to him,*
and he will make your paths straight.

ONE DAY I caught my son stealing gummy bears. He dashed out of the kitchen, leaving the bag of bears upended on the counter. I turned the corner to the living room and there he was, my little man, hiding under the couch with his legs dangling out. I couldn't help but laugh. He's like every other little kid: somehow convinced that if they can't see you, you can't see them. He's just like us. We do the same with God.

My smile faded as I thought about how deeply I wanted my boy to know two things:

1. I can see you. I know what you did, and it doesn't change my love for you.
2. And I can see what you did (sin), and I can see what it's doing to you.

165

That's why I wanted to talk to him about the bear-stealing incident. I didn't want to shame him, but he needed to know something important: my love doesn't change with his behavior. I wanted my love to do what love does: move him toward desiring something better. The love I have for my boy meets him where he is but doesn't want to leave him there.

"Foster? Come on out, buddy."

No response. He darted for his room without even looking back at me. I could relate. I've run into my bedroom without looking back when my heavenly Father called my name. I could imagine myself cleaning up the entire bedroom, mopping even, so that by the time God got there, He would be proud of me again.

Knowing this, I walked into my boy's bedroom. I was still proud of him because he's mine. I wanted him to know that I knew *everything* and still loved him. Of course, God knows everything already. But we hide because we don't want to submit to His omniscience. If you're only 95 percent known, you're still unknown. You won't be able to receive the love of God fully because you're still hiding that percentage of you. You can't receive love fully if you're not fully known.

J. I. Packer beautifully articulates this in his book *Knowing God*.

What matters supremely, therefore, is not, in the last analysis, the fact that I know God, but the larger fact which underlies it—the fact that he knows me. I am graven on the palms of his hands [Isa. 49:16]. I am never out of his mind. All my knowledge of him depends on his sustained initiative in knowing me. I know him because he first knew me, and continues to know me. He knows me as a friend, one who loves me; and there is no moment when his eye is off me, or his attention distracted from me, and no moment, therefore, when his care falters.

This is momentous knowledge. There is unspeakable comfort—the sort of comfort that energizes, be it said, not enervates—in knowing that God is constantly taking knowledge of me in love and watching over me for my good. There is tremendous relief in knowing that his love to me is utterly realistic, based at every point on prior knowledge of the worst about me, so that no discovery now can disillusion him about me, in the way I am so often disillusioned about myself, and quench his determination to bless me.[28]

God knows *all* of you. He sees all of you. He sees all of it and knows, more than you ever will, what it is doing to you. He wants to look into your little face and say, "You can talk to Me about all of it. I love you. I'm with you. I'm not going anywhere." It took me and my boy fifteen minutes to land there. I sat in his doorway while he hid under his bed.

"You can come out now."

"Nuh-uh. Don't want to."

"I know you wanna hide. I understand wanting to do that, but you can tell me everything because I love you."

Silence.

"You don't have to deal with anything on your own. You can tell me. Did you steal the gummy bears?"

More silence.

"I get it, buddy. I wouldn't want to talk about it either. But did you maybe, kind of, possibly steal the gummy bears?"

Even more silence.

After a while, he crawled over to the doorway and put his head in my lap. "Mama, I maybe took a bunch of gummy bears."

"I'm so glad you told me."

He finally (maybe) confessed, "Maybe I kinda *did* take the gummy bears. I'm sorry."

"I forgive you."

God already knows what you're going to tell Him, but He still wants to talk about it. That impulse to hide is, at its root, an unwillingness to go to God. It's an attempt to "figure it all out" or clean ourselves up (which ends up being more of a covering than a cleaning) to somehow feel more presentable. In Psalm 51, King David shows us another way to look at mistakes. He let his guilt turn him to God instead of leaning on himself. Leaning on himself hadn't worked in the past, and it won't work ever. David saw his sin (verse 3: "For I know my transgressions, and my sin is always before me"), and he took it to God. This is part of what it means to be "a man after God's own heart." David was literally after God's heart. Whatever he was holding in his hands, he carried it toward God.

Do you see your sin? Seeing your sin is a gift.

Modern medicine has created incredible technology called MRI scanners, which scan the body to find out where a tumor or any sort of sickness is. This is useful and important because we need to know where the sickness is to have a chance at finding healing. So let me invite you to see yourself. Do you see the judgmental side of yourself? Your pride? All the things you want to hide from Him? Your mistakes? Solomon reminds us in Proverbs 3:6 that in all our ways, even our mistakes, we can submit to God.

Let me forewarn you: it's going to be tempting to do a shallow cleanup (cover-up) and walk away from this chapter not having been transformed. Seeing your sin is uncomfortable, but it's the only way to be transformed.

I know some of you believe that seeing your sin is in no way a gift. And some of you don't see your sin much at all. I've been in both camps. I've been horrified at the ugliness of my sin, and I've also done my level best to ignore it. I'd argue that both of these approaches have the same root—ahem, autonomy—and that neither of those ways constitutes submission to God. And when we don't submit all our ways to God, the result is pain. But when we submit ourselves to God, as uncomfortable as it might seem, we open ourselves up to receiving love and healing. Hiding will result in something even worse than the original mistake, but opening ourselves to God will result in something even better than we ever dreamed: redemption. That means that God will take our mistake, this ugly thing we want to hide, and in ways that we can't even begin to imagine or dream possible, will use those mistakes to make us new. When you put it like that, it seems like a pretty easy choice, doesn't it?

So how do we submit our mistakes to Him?

We come out of hiding, trusting in His promise to forgive us and transform us.

THE MIDDLE OF THE ROOM

When my boys were in diapers, I rarely changed them on a changing table. I always thought I'd utilize the cute little dresser with the cute little changing pad next to a cute diaper genie. Nope. When a boy needs to get changed, we change him right where he is. Playing in the back yard? Playing inside with blocks? Sure, we change him there. By the pool? Yep. On the rug? Why not? He needs it! On our white couch? *Of course not.* Who do you think I am?

The truth: cleaning has never been my highest priority. This is probably why Randy laughed when he opened an Amazon box to find that I'd ordered a duster. For the record, I needed it for a sermon illustration, not for deep cleaning. Deep cleaning was never on my to-do list. He held it up to look at it and asked me, "Do these things even work? I mean, think about what it does. It just moves the dust to somewhere else."

How weird would it be if I invited you to come over to my house and I had left a dirty diaper there in the middle of the living room? Do you want to know what would be even weirder? If, while there was a dirty diaper in the middle of the living room, I was holding a duster, apologizing for the state of the house, and frantically trying to clean the dust off the piano in the corner of the room. You'd think I was nuts for focusing on dust. *Megan, there's a load of crap in the middle of the room.* It would also be weird if I saw the dirty diaper, fell to my knees, and started apologizing for the absolutely awful horror you had to witness without attempting to do anything about it. *It's okay, Megan, calm down. You could just take the diaper to the outside trash.*

So what are you going to do with the crap in the middle of your room?

Will you open your heart to your mistakes right here as you read these pages? Will you open them to the Lord and acknowledge Him in this way? Will you ask Him to reveal the sin underneath those sins (what's happening in your heart)?

I mean, why do we even sin? It happens when we don't acknowledge God in all our ways.

You may be struggling with lust, and I wonder if God is revealing your heart as lonely.

Do you gossip because you feel left out and not pursued?

Why are you so angry? Is there something you're afraid of?

Is there any place in your life you're being dishonest about? Where are you pretending to be more spiritual than you are?

I'm not asking these questions to shame you but to invite you into greater freedom. God knows it all, and remember, He knows what it's doing to you, so of course, He wants to bring it up. If we open up the behavior to God, He can reveal our hearts. Why do we sin in this way? Is the deeper longing a harmful longing in general or a necessary longing that needs to be met in a truly satisfying way? This is what it means to acknowledge God in our mistakes.

For those of you who feel stuck, I want you to know that there is a third option—besides "grab the duster" (ignore your sin) or "weep over the diaper" (obsess about your sin). It's confession. It's taking that diaper to the trash. It's going to God with your sin, relinquishing your autonomy, and telling Him, "Here's what happened." Confession is liberating, not crushing. To confess means "to agree with." You're getting on the same page with God about what happened, just like when my son finally maybe told me about the gummy bears.

"Lord, I realize I'm not as I should be." That's not a surprise to Him or me. And He has plans for me to grow. We just need to acknowledge Him, to let our sin lead us to His heart for us. It's His love that led Him to offer grace—unmerited favor. We don't have to respond to our mistakes by trying to earn His favor. Earning something that is unmerited is illogical. It wouldn't be grace if it could be earned. But it is grace, and it's there for the taking.

God is pursuing your failure with an unfailing love. Jesus took your sin. Come broken; be healed. Come thirsty; leave satisfied. God doesn't want to ignore your sin; He wants to rewrite it for His glory. There's nothing too dark, nothing too bad. Remember the cross and stop hiding your mistakes from it. Tim Keller says, "We are more sinful and flawed in ourselves than we ever dared believe, yet at the very same time we are more loved and accepted in Jesus Christ than we ever dared hope."[29]

What will you do with your guilt and shame and mistakes? God loves you knowing all of you. Don't lean on your own understanding. Don't lean on yourself.

Lean on His grace.

"I Forgive You"

I've learned a lot about my relationship with the Lord through my relationship with my own kids. I've learned about grace and forgiveness. Whenever one of my boys would slug the other one, I used to force the hitter to say "I'm sorry" before they ran off, not thinking twice about it. They did their job and apologized, right? But it didn't feel like enough. The boy who was hit would sit there and be thrown another blow through an unrepentant "I'm sorry." Quickly, I realized that they at least needed to add what they were sorry for. Why do we do that? We need to realize the truth. It's important to name the truth of what you're sorry for. "I'm sorry I hit you, bye."

It still wasn't enough. It still felt like another thing thrown at the injured little guy. Recently, we added one final step to our apology rhythm: "I'm sorry for [blank]. *Will you forgive me?*" What happens in that moment, the moment you ask for forgiveness? You take the power and you put it in the hands of the one who has been harmed. And then the one who was harmed holds the power to forgive.

So does God forgive us?

Yes.

All of us?

Yes.

Even the ones who [insert the worst thing you can think of here].

We're all forgiven. All of us. No matter what. But we have a hard time believing we're forgiven.

Believing in His capacity to forgive us is a great way to submit our mistakes to Him. What does our response look like when we believe in His forgiveness? We open "our ways" and the heart behind them to the reality of Christ's finished work on the cross and the presence of the Holy Spirit. If our sins are truly attributed to Christ on the cross and there's no condemnation for those who are in Him, then we can come out of hiding.

Be honest. Tell God everything. It won't surprise Him. His Holy Spirit will lead us to freedom as our mistakes lead us to declare, "Oh Lord, how I need You." God delights in our reliance upon His Spirit in our weakness. It's where His power can be revealed.

We're totally accepted by the Father through the Son because His righteousness has been attributed to us. We can stop trying to cover our badness with our goodness. No amount of being good can cleanse our shame and guilt; only Christ Jesus can do that. So let Him! If the Holy Spirit is the actual agent of growth, you can stop leaning on yourself. You can stop trying to quit making the same mistakes in the power of the self alone. There's another option: let your mistakes lead you to God. He wants to mature you. He knows and wants what's best for you. When we hide, we forget God's movement toward us in love. So come to Him.

Go to God.

SEARCH MY HEART

Let me be specific with what it looks like for me.

Before I step up to speak at a church or have a difficult conversation with a friend, I try to remember that God first wants to meet me right where I am—no need for a sudden surge of holiness. I don't have to put on a facade of being happier or less angry than I am in that moment. God meets me where I am, and my goal is to open my heart wide for that divine connection.

I draw a heart and extend spokes from it. In a moment of quiet reflection, I invite God to search my heart. Words, emotions, mistakes, grief, people—anything that surfaces gets jotted down, each attached to a spoke. "Tired. Excited. Insecure. Worried about making everything all about me. Shameful about a mistake. Concerned for my son. Curious about lunch."

Once I fill up the spokes, I take another spin around the wheel of my heart with God. I write a sentence about each concern, then open my mind and heart to God to remind me of something true, penning it down. Then I let God help me weave the two together to form the third sentence.

"Tired: God, I'm doing too much. I know You're always working. Help me rest in Your work instead of feeling bogged down by mine."

"Concerned for my son: God, I don't know how to control him. You love him. Help me love him like You do, without trying to control the uncontrollable."

"Shameful about a mistake: God, I'm so sorry. You've forgiven me. Help me live free."

Every time I share my heart with God, His heart meets mine in that sacred exchange. While sharing my heart doesn't change the situation, finding God's heart often transforms my heart toward it. Relax; He's in control. You're fully forgiven and accepted already.

Opening the heart and sharing everything in there takes time and honest dialogue. In prayer, the mistakes must be named and the heart must be explored as we make the first move and go to God.

The second move is to live differently because of the grace of God. Remember, though, the order here is everything. The first move is to go to God and come out of hiding as you verbalize what is in your heart. And you don't have to do this alone. He will come running to you with arms full of unearned love and life-changing grace. Our behaviors can be changed by His love, but we need to go to Him first!

Too many books and sermons spend all the time in the

world on the second move—living differently. The problem is that we usually try to live differently without God. This sounds ridiculous, but we do it all the time. Too often we would rather jump into step two and try to live better, figuring if we got ourselves into this mess, we should be responsible for getting ourselves out of it. That's a lie. Instead, go to God! Don't perform for Him, be with Him.

Hardly anyone wakes up wanting to make a whole lot of bad choices that day. God knows this because He knows our hearts, the wellspring of our behavior. Our mistakes are rooted in our hearts. God wants to transform our desires not by changing our behavior but by addressing our hearts. This is why the first step cannot be modifying our behavior, because the healing that we need begins in the heart. True healing takes place as we open our hearts in prayer. What's going on inside your heart?

Imagine a water bottle. If you shake an uncapped water bottle full of water, what comes out? Water. Why does water come out? There are two reasons:

1. Because you shook it
2. Because there was water on the inside

Do you want to know why you've acted out in anger lately? You got angry not just because something shook you but because anger was already there on the inside. Anger is in your heart. We don't fix the heart by just trying. "Stop being so angry, self!" Instead, we need to look inside the water bottle and see what's in there. "Whoa, that thing is filled up to the brim. What's going on?" Let God look at your heart with you. He is all knowing, kind and patient, and oh so tender with you and your heart. Even though you've been trying for years to "just not be so angry," the contents of your heart spill out every time your life is shaken (when tragedy strikes, when you're cut off on the free-way, when your kids disobey). This is because fixing our hearts is a process, not a one-time decision.

What's been coming out of your life lately? Is it anger? Big mistakes? Loneliness leading to lust? Annoyance? Envy? Pride? Whatever is coming out of your heart—ahem, all of your behav-ior—is a result of whatever is already in your heart in the first place. If you're angry, tell Him. Ask Him to help you understand why. If you're disappointed with yourself and feeling hopeless, tell Him. If you don't care about anything, tell Him. If you can't seem to forgive yourself, tell Him. Wherever you're at is right where He wants to be.

We tend to want to pray for magic: "God, take away my worry" or "Help me stop making this same mistake." And these are okay prayers. At some point, though, we need to let God work in the deep places of the heart, the places where the mistakes are coming from. Honest prayer can crack open our hearts to help us understand why worry is there in the first place or why we act entitled in our behavior or talk poorly about others. The worry or pride or jealousy has somehow formed in our hearts over time, and it will be transformed over time too.

There are practical reasons why the process takes time. If I asked God to take away my worry in an instant, and then He did, I would start walking down far too many dark alleys by myself (literally and metaphorically). God gave us the capacity to fear and worry and be angry and not sin. At some point, we need to open our hearts and our worries and fears and mistakes to God. Yes, we all make mistakes, but we can't let the darkness separate us from our loving God. We need to go to God with the truth first. He's not surprised.

God dwells within us, and at just the right time, He lets us see what is coming out of our hearts through our behaviors and mistakes. In that moment we have a choice: try to jump to step two and change our behavior, or stick with step one: go to God.

Opening your heart to Him is going to lead to surprise, not shame. I'm serious. Maybe you've been angry lately—really angry. In anger, you've lashed out and hurt others. When you open up your anger to the Holy Spirit, you might be surprised to find that God is angry too—but not at you. He's angry about the source of your anger. He hates injustice. He knows how to be angry without making mistakes.

Some of you have been angry for years, and God, in His lovingkindness, is letting you see your anger yet again because He wants to transform your anger by His love and grace. We'll forgive others only when we open our hearts to the truth of our resentments, anger, and hatred toward self and others and see God's lovingkindness toward us in the moments we don't deserve it. Only then will we ever have the ability to extend that love to others who don't deserve it either.

Look at your life: Are you angrier than you'd like to admit? Making all kinds of mistakes that you never thought you'd make? What has been splashing out of your water bottle? If it's guilt, let the Holy Spirit look at it with you. He'll lead you to the cross where you can find the forgiveness you need. His tone is kind and compassionate. His character is just and loving. Our mistakes can help us know God's life-transforming love and grace.

Go to God.

No amount of knowing the right way to live is going to be powerful enough to cause you to live differently. Your prayer can be, "God, what are You revealing about my heart through my mistakes?" Instead of praying for God to take them all away, allow God to crack open your heart and reveal them so that He might begin the powerful process of transformation, not just momentary behavior modification.

In sum, don't skip step one. Go to God so that He can begin to transform the heart or resolve the deep beliefs and desires of the heart. We tend to focus on the good (what we should become) and seldom pay attention to the bad. This makes sense; seeing our bad can make us feel shame and guilt. But God has a different plan—He asks us to submit our mistakes to Him. In doing so, we find out that His love has never depended on our performance. Thanks be to God.

Once, when I was scrolling Instagram, I came across this gem: "Anytime I ever broke a dish, my mom would holler from the other room, 'I love you more than that dish.' No lecture. No shame. No eye-rolling. Just wild, undeserved—GRACE."[30] God, through His Word, shouts the same sort of thing.

"I love you more than your mistakes."

No lecture.

No shame.

No eye-rolling.

Just wild, undeserved grace.

GO TO GOD

Childlike Approach

God asks us to be childlike.

I don't think He's asking us to hide under the couch, but I do think He wants us to come to Him with our mistakes. And since He's a loving, all-knowing Father, He understands why we hide the way we do.

Let's go to Him right now. Let Him bring one of your mistakes to mind. Maybe not a "big" one but something you need to talk about with Him.

You can talk to Him about anything, you know.

As simply as you can, say the mistake. You don't have to hide it, ignore it, or elaborate on it.

Just say it, and then write it down.

Then know two things:

1. His love for you hasn't changed.
2. He knows what your sin is doing to you, and He doesn't want you to hurt anymore.

How do you want to respond to Him?

4
PART

*And He Will Make
Your Paths Straight*

CHAPTER 12

HE WILL MAKE YOUR
PATHS STRAIGHT

Trust in the LORD with all your heart
and lean not on your own understanding;
in all your ways submit to him,
and he will make your paths straight.

I LOVE DANCING. I even used to be on the hip-hop dance team in college. The only downside to years of onstage performances was adapting to dancing with my husband. At first, I thought we didn't dance well together because he didn't want to dance. It wasn't until years into marriage that he confessed, "It's not that I don't like dancing, it's just that you tend to dance *at* me instead of *with* me." I can laugh at this now. You can laugh with me too: imagine me moonwalking toward and away from him, right in the middle of a circle he never wished to be a part of in the first place. When he told me this, I wasn't laughing. I was more embarrassed. I was also bummed he wasn't more impressed.

Dancing with a person and walking with God share remarkable parallels. Both require trust, connection, and surrender. Just as two dancers move together in harmonious rhythm, anticipating each other's steps and responding to subtle cues, our spiritual growth involves a graceful interplay with God. We don't perform in our Christian lives *at* God, to impress Him, to make Him proud of us or love us more; we walk *with* Him, trusting He's already proud of us. Plus, we can be confident and relaxed because He's the one leading the dance. We can surrender the illusion of control and its consequential burdens. And just like a bride on her wedding day, we have a part to play. Our part in the faith-filled dance with God is the bride who confidently follows her groom's lead on the dance floor. His leading serves as her guide. And her following shows that she is with Him and trusts His leading. The relationship between our role and God's role in our spiritual growth is the dance between our efforts and divine grace. As Dallas Willard says, "Grace is not opposed to effort, it is opposed to earning. Earning is an attitude. Effort is an action. Grace, you know, does not just have to do with forgiveness of sins alone."[31]

Grace is unmerited favor. While grace can't be earned (otherwise it wouldn't be grace), it does move us. We live differently as the Holy Spirit enables us to receive Christ and the benefits of His grace. Our efforts and divine grace are synergistic. As Proverbs 3:5–6 encourages our part, it concludes with God's part:

> Trust in the LORD with all your heart
> and lean not on your own
> understanding;
> in all your ways submit to him,
> and he will make your paths
> straight.

"He will." Did you catch that? In the end, *God will* make our paths straight. In other words, we will change not because we try hard to change but because we try hard to trust in the one who can change us. The verses are so straightforward. Do this, not this, in all your ways, and then He will do this.

I think some of us would be more comfortable if the verses went more like this: "I do this, I don't do that, I do this in all my ways, and then it will all be good (I'll be comfortable, successful, and rich, plus I will have it all figured out)." Nope. It doesn't say, "We will make our paths straight through our effort." He will. He will make our paths straight because He knows the path. And the path He is taking us on is one that forms us more into His likeness.

So what is God's part in this dance, and what is our part?

Sanctification (growth into Christlikeness) is synergistic. While it's not all up to you, God absolutely works cooperatively *with* you. The apostle Paul's words in Philippians 2:12–13 beautifully capture this dance: "Therefore, my dear friends, as you have always obeyed—not only in my presence, but now much more in my absence—continue to work out your salvation with fear and trembling, for it is God who works in you to will and to act in order to fulfill his good purpose." You ought to work, for it is God who works in you.

If you're not a dancer, let's try a metaphor popularly attributed to St. Augustine. He writes, "God provides the wind, man must raise the sail." This metaphor eloquently illustrates the relationship between our efforts (raising the sail) and God's guiding influence (providing the wind) in our spiritual growth. This is what Paul is getting at when, in Ephesians, he tells us to "be filled with the Holy Spirit" (5:18 NLT). Such an interesting choice of words: a passive imperative. A passive imperative is a command for you to do something, but rather than you being the doer, you're to *let* something be done *to* you. So much of the dance with divine grace involves opening ourselves and our lives and all the things to His grace to *let* something happen to us. To let Him transform. To let grace overwhelm. To be humbled. Check out the following verses and see if you can identify the two members of the dance:

- Psalm 37:5: "Commit your way to the LORD; trust in him, and he will act" (ESV).
- James 4:8: "Come near to God and he will come near to you."
- Colossians 1:29: "To this end I strenuously contend with all the energy Christ so powerfully works in me."
- Psalm 127:1: "Unless the LORD builds the house, the builders labor in vain. Unless the LORD watches over the city, the guards stand watch in vain."
- 1 Corinthians 3:6–7: "I planted the seed, Apollos watered it, but God has been making it grow. So neither the one who plants nor the one who waters is anything, but only God, who makes things grow."
- Ephesians 2:8–10: "For it is by grace you have been saved, through faith—and this is not from yourselves, it is the gift of God—not by works, so that no one can boast. For we are God's handiwork, created in Christ Jesus to do good works, which God prepared in advance for us to do."

Jesus Himself speaks to the dance in John 15:4–5: "Abide in me, and I in you. As the branch cannot bear fruit by itself, unless it abides in the vine, neither can you, unless you abide in me. I am the vine; you are the branches. Whoever abides in me and I in him, he it is that bears much fruit, for apart from me you can do nothing" (ESV). Christ illustrates that our fruitful living is dependent upon our connection to Him, while also underscoring the necessity of our abiding. In other words, we don't produce life on our own. That comes only through connection to Him. But we do have to stay connected. This is our part in the dance.

In what seems to be a paraphrase of the words from St. Augustine's 169th sermon, Robert E. Luccock writes, "Without God, we cannot. Without us, God will not."[32] The way we bear the fruit of the Holy Spirit is not through our effort. Love, joy, peace, patience, kindness, goodness, gentleness, faithfulness, and self-control are not the fruit of our effort but the fruit of His Spirit. Us in Him (abiding), and Him in us (bearing fruit). As we take steps toward our part of the dance by opening to God through prayer, study of God's Word, worship, and acts of service, the gracious hand of God transforms us from within. Our part, therefore, is a journey of humility, obedience, and trust in God, sharing the truth of our hearts with Him while participating fully in the sanctification process. We find His hold on us as we hold on to Him.

Randy and I used to live downtown and walk everywhere. Over every alleyway, he would consistently tell our son Foster to hold his hand tightly. Every single alley we crossed began with the two of them pausing and Randy reminding Foster to grab his hand. The truth was, though, it didn't matter how tightly Foster held Randy's hand. Why? Because Randy was holding his.

The world tells us that the highest virtue is independence, but Scripture tells us that *He* will make your paths straight. He was already working before you picked up this book, and He will work after you finish it. While you can't figure it all out or grow yourself by yourself, you do have a role to play. You don't have to have the answers; but thankfully, you're growing in honest relationship with the one who does.

As we wrap up this book, we can no longer attempt to grow ourselves by ourselves. Instead, we must join the dance!

So where do we begin? Proverbs 3:5–6.

Trust in the LORD with all your heart
and lean not on your own
understanding;
in all your ways submit to him,
and he will make your paths
straight.

Let's walk through this practically. In the middle of listening to a sermon, when your conscious is pricked and you think, *Oh, I should do that better*, go to God instead of yourself. Don't make plans to "do better"—join the dance! As we share honestly with God whatever is on our hearts, our hearts get closer to His. His heart gets closer to ours. Practically, going to God may sound similar to this. Imagine yourself in church. It's that moment again—you hear something that resonates with you and convicts you, something that compels you toward change:

1. *Trust in the Lord with all your heart.* Remember who you can trust, the one who loves you the most. Share what God brings to mind when your conscience is pricked. Tell Him, "God, I want to get better at this," or, "I'm mad that I keep struggling," or, "I'm sad [or confused or hopeful]."

2. *Lean not on your own understanding.* Remember whom you can lean on, the one who knows you and His path for you the most. Admit you can't know everything and find freedom leaning on the omniscience and presence and love of God. "God, I don't need to understand everything. Give me faith to trust You instead. I also know I won't get better at this on my own. I need You. You understand both me and the circumstances I'm facing. You have a plan to grow me. Use this to form me more into Your likeness."

3. *He will make your paths straight.* Remember who is leading the dance, the one who isn't worried about a thing.
   He is thoughtfully, carefully, and lovingly guiding you
   toward His heart and the things He has prepared in
   advance for you to do as you become more like Him. So
   wait and listen for how He might lead you to respond.
   "God, what would You have me say, know, or do in
   response to Your Spirit at work in me?"

In all your ways and thoughts and emotions and trials and
griefs and relationships and mistakes, open up to God, and He
will . . . do whatever He wishes. He will direct your path. He
may lead you to confession of sin. He may bring Scripture to
mind. He may lead you to forgive someone. He may lead you to
ask someone to go to lunch. He may lead you to do unto others
as you would have them do unto you (Matt. 7:12), "mourn with
those who mourn" (Rom. 12:15), or cast all your cares on Him
because He cares for you (1 Peter 5:7). The more you know His
Word, the more familiar His voice will become. The more open
you are to the life of Christ already in you, the more your desires
become His.

Know that the path He is taking you on begins as your heart
gets closer to His. While I can't tell you where He might direct
you, I can tell you that whatever He will have you say, know,
believe, or do will be loving. He may not tell you what to do
(although I know that He loves to give hints), but He will form
you more into His likeness (remember, He is love) so that you
can do what you believe He would do if He were you.

The reason we can relax in the dance of sanctification is
because He's leading. How wonderful that the answer is found
not in some prescription for our actions but instead in what
Christ is doing in us. It's His life in us. He's leading the dance.
The question we end up with may no longer be "God what

should I do?" but rather "God, what are You already doing, and how can I join You?"

The path He is leading us on is full of the works He has "prepared in advance" for us to do. We can take a breath and relax.

To see sanctification as something that Christ is doing and will do in me as I trust Him with my heart and submit my ways to His, both humbles me and makes me more relaxed when it comes to my own spiritual growth. *He will* direct my path as I *let* Him.

WHERE DOES THE PATH GO?

Proverbs 3:5–6 ends with "and he will make your paths straight." This means that, when we trust in the Lord and stop relying on our own ways, but instead rely on God (acknowledging Him by opening all our ways and decisions to Him), He will guide us on the path. Now, before you quote these verses to a friend, be sure to make it clear that God may not give direct revelation about what they need to do in a specific instance. Rather, He's spiritually forming us to become the type of people who can make Christlike decisions. This is important. God is interested in maturing us to become the kind of people who know what He wants instead of constantly needing to be told what to do or not to do. This is why our sanctification, our growth in becoming more like Him, is more important than mere behavior modification. Christ is forming the deep wellspring of our behaviors through His will.

Many of us imagine God's will for our lives as a bull's-eye to hit.[33] Should I marry this person? Should I apply for that job? We feel the urgency to hit the center dot and find God's will. What if God's will for your life is less about hitting the center of an imaginary bull's-eye and more about learning to become a Christlike chooser? This is Romans 12:2: "Do not conform to the pattern of this world, but be transformed by the renewing of your mind. *Then you will be able to test and approve what God's will is—his good, pleasing and perfect will*" (emphasis added). Maybe the goal is not to have a perfect record of our thirty-five thousand choices each day but instead to become the type of people (formed into Christlikeness) who make God-honoring choices about whom to marry, whom to notice at a gathering, how to work hard ethically, and how to love others generously. God will give us wisdom in our choosing.

His direction in our lives is comprehensive—He can see the whole picture, and He doesn't leave anything out (are you convinced that He's the better dance leader yet?). After Paul shares "We know that in all things God works for the good of those who love him, who have been called according to his purpose" (Rom. 8:28), he defines in the next verse what he means by "good": "For those God foreknew he also predestined to be conformed to the image of his Son." The good God is doing in all things is forming us more into the likeness of Jesus, the Son.[34] We can relax, because He has predestined us to be conformed, and His means for conforming us is all the things in our lives as we open them to Him. That is the good God is doing in all things. Recall Paul's words in Galatians 4:19: "My dear children, for whom I am again in the pains of childbirth until *Christ is formed in you*" (emphasis added). Paul was saying to the spiritually young Galatian church, "I long for the day when Christ is formed in you." He longed for this as a mother would long for the birth of her child. Like Paul, I find myself longing for the day when Christ is formed in me and in my kids and in my friends and in you.

Not only did Paul want us to be formed into Christlikeness, but Jesus prayed for it in John 17. He didn't pray just for His disciples. Remember: "My prayer is not for them alone. I pray also for those who will believe in me through their message" (v. 20). *That's us!* Get ready, because this is His prayer for us: "That all of them may be one, Father, just as you are in me and I am in you. May they also be in us so that the world may believe that you have sent me. I have given them the glory that you gave me, that they may be one as we are one—*I in them and you in me*— so that they may be brought to complete unity. Then the world will know that you sent me and have loved them *even as* you have loved me" (vv. 21–23, emphases added).

Jesus prayed to His Father that we might become unified not only with others but also with Him. He prayed that the path we would walk would lead us to be one with Him and others so the world could know that He was sent by the Father to love us all. He longs for us to be close to Him, walking the path He has for us, resulting in our becoming more like Him by His Holy Spirit at work in us. We know this because He prayed for His love to transform us.

To understand this even better, let's go back to the image used in Proverbs 3:6—the image of a path. In Old Testament times, roads were rough at best and dangerous at worst. Travel was exhausting and treacherous. When a king took a journey, some of his servants would go ahead of his caravan to smooth the rough places and remove the obstacles in the road. They would make his paths straight. This image is used to describe John the Baptist's role in relation to the coming of Jesus: "A voice of one calling: 'In the wilderness prepare the way for the LORD; make straight in the desert a highway for our God. Every valley shall be raised up, every mountain and hill made low; the rough ground shall become level, the rugged places a plain'" (Isa. 40:3–4).

"And he will make your paths straight" is also translated "and He will direct your paths" (MEV). It's important to grasp this phrase in the context of Proverbs 3:5–6. It's a conditional statement. *If* we submit to Him in all ways, *then* He will make our paths straight.

This isn't to say the Lord is going to remove all the obstacles in our lives; it's closer to meaning that we can have faith that our paths will be laid out before us. The issue is we think the only way we can have peace is by knowing the paths before we walk them.

But that's not faith.

Making straight paths is intimately connected to the idea of preparing the way for the Lord. To make straight paths is an *extension* of what it means to prepare the way for the Lord.

Trust in the Lord with all your heart. Don't hide or cover a thing. Lay it all out before the one who loves you. He'll meet you there and not ever leave you there by yourself. He'll walk with you as you renounce self-reliance, as you lean not on your own understanding. Rather, acknowledge God everywhere. Then He will make your paths straight. He'll align your desires with His. Your sinful desires will feel uncomfortable in His presence. Your Christlike choices will feel like fruit. Our lives will look like love, joy, and peace.

THE FRUIT

But what does letting Him direct your paths look like in real life?

To answer that, I'm going to have to take you to Olive Garden.

I love Olive Garden.

Sorry to anyone who doesn't like Olive Garden. I realize that this can be kind of a polarizing subject. Some, like me, love it; others call it the McDonald's of Italian food. When I was pregnant with my second son, Jed, I craved Italian food *all the time*. There was an Olive Garden nearby, so we became regulars. Then after Jed was born, I realized I just really like Italian food. So I never stopped going to Olive Garden.

I order the soup and salad combo.

Yeeeesss.

It's bottomless soup, salad, and breadsticks.

The best is that moment when the server sees that I'm done with my first round of soup and asks, "Do you want another bowl of soup?"

And I say yes. Then the same thing happens with the second bowl. And then I say, "You know what, I'll just try all of them." Then they bring me a bowl of every single soup simmering in the kitchen that day. Did you know you could do that? Now you do.

About a year ago I was speaking in Nashville, Tennessee. After the speaking engagement was over, I stayed for a night by myself before traveling back home. I was in the downtown area, surrounded by Tennessee's most glorious food offerings, restaurants that critics raved about, so I pulled out my phone and googled, "Where is Olive Garden?"

Fortunately, they had one in Nashville too. Otherwise, I would have had to improvise. When I walked in, the host asked me, "How many in your party?" I just kind of waved at him.

"Hey, it's me, just me. I'm the party."

Of course, it wasn't just me. It was me and Jesus, and we were going to Olive Garden for some time together. I knew what we were going to order—the soup and salad combo for one. Our waitress was not great. Maybe she wasn't having the best evening for any number of reasons. This night was not her night for exemplary waitressing. Megan trivia: I was a waitress for seven years, so I know what it looks like when things are going well and when things aren't.

After I'd been sitting there at my table for one (two, actually!) for a bit, she came by to take my order.

"I'm gonna do the soup and salad combo, starting with the Soupa Zuppa!" This is what I call the Zuppa Toscana, this delicious soup with sausage and kale, and usually Olive Garden waitstaff think the joke is funny, or at least they laugh for my sake, but my waitress didn't laugh.

After a while, she brought back the bowl of soup, set it down, and hurried away to one of her other tables. I gave a sincere but short "Thank you for this" to the one sitting across the table from me, and then I surveyed the feast—soup, breadsticks, and salad (I don't usually eat that part). Everything was there except for a spoon. And a glass of water.

But you know what? It was all okay. I was there to spend time with Jesus. When she came by again, I asked her about a spoon. She apologized, told me they were down a waitress, and ran back to the kitchen for a spoon, but she didn't come back. So I pulled one of the bussers aside and asked for a spoon. I figured that was more important than the water.

The meal went on like this. She never asked if I wanted more soup, but that was okay, too, because I was with Him, and that was enough. I even picked at the salad for a little bit—not bad, but not really my thing.

"Okay, what is your deal?"

I looked up from my salad. It was my waitress. "Huh? Me? My deal?" I asked.

"What is your deal? There's something different about you."

"Yeah?"

"Yeah. I mean, I never even took your drink order. But you didn't complain, and you weren't nasty to me, and you just . . . you're different. What's your deal?"

I laughed. "I know the answer to that question. Did I come across as loving by chance?"

"Yeah. Yeah, you did."

"Or maybe joyful and peaceful?"

"Uh-huh."

"Or patient and kind?"

She just looked at me. Maybe she was thinking at this point, *Kind of arrogant too*. But I kept going.

"Did I come across as gentle and self-controlled, maybe?" I walked down the list of the fruit of the Spirit. Her response was a nod and a confused expression. I looked into her eyes and said, "Any of that—loving, patient, gentle—is Christ in me. It's not me. Let me confess to you, by nature, I'm not that loving. I'm extremely selfish. I love to be loved back. I'm not all that joyful. Some days, I want my earbuds in and to be in the corner all by myself. Most days, I'm hurried and busy and distracted. I know the answer to your question. What's my deal? Why am I different? If anything is different about me, it's Jesus."

After her shift was done, she sat at that table for one (now three!) with me, and she met Jesus for the first time.

When He's directing your path, you get to be the light to other people—bad waitresses, people who cut you off in the church parking lot, disobedient kids. You open your heart to the whole world, one person at a time. Which person? Whichever person He's placed in your path that day. He's directing their path too.

Let Him do whatever He desires on the path He's taking you that will inevitably lead you to becoming more like Him, for your sake and for the sake of the world. Every person you meet, every moment you live, every situation you ever find yourself in can open you to a real conversation with God about your real life. And when you're sharing your life with God, you're walking with Him. He will direct your paths as you bring your heart closer to His, as He transforms it by the power of the Holy Spirit, so that you might become more like Him.

Don't worry.

He's not worried.

You can relax. *He will* lead the dance. He always does.

He Will

God's invitation to follow Him assumes He is already moving.

Sometimes I feel the need to start something or be the source of something profound.

I have a gift for you here in the conclusion of this book. You don't have to start something new. You're invited to open your heart through honest prayer and join in on the good work that God has already begun. Rather than asking, "God what would You have me do?" ask, "God, what are You already doing?"

Follow that up with "And how can I join You?"

Let's dance!

NOTES

1. Bill Gaultiere, "A Simple Solution to Stress from Dallas Willard," Soul Shepherding, May 2021, www.soulshepherding .org/a-simple-solution-to-stress-from-dallas-willard/.
2. Rom. 8:26–27, 34; 1 John 2:1; Heb. 7:25; John 17:20–26.
3. Peter Scazzero, "The Problem of Emotionally Unhealthy Spirituality," part 1 in *Emotionally Healthy Spirituality* (Nashville: Thomas Nelson, 2006).
4. He got the job.
5. Bill Gaultiere, *Your Best Life in Jesus' Easy Yoke: Rhythms of Grace to De-stress and Live Empowered*, updated ed. (2010; repr., Irvine, CA: Soul Shepherding, 2020), 4.
6. John Coe, "Spiritual Moralism" (lecture, Talbot School of Theology, La Mirada, CA, June 2023).
7. All of this "hidden heart" content is taken from lectures Dr. Coe gave during my doctorate course and his freestanding article, *The Hidden Heart—Why We Still Sin When We Know So Much*, 2004, digitalcommons.biola.edu /cgi/viewcontent.cgi?filename=2&article=1003&context=isf -lect-pre&type=additional. It would be impossible to overstate how influential Dr. Coe's teaching has been on this book— he's the one who got me thinking about autonomy in the first place.

8. Martin Luther, *The Bondage of the Will*, trans. J. I. Packer and O. R. Johnston (1525; repr., Grand Rapids: Baker Academic, 2012).

9. John Flavel, *Keeping the Heart: A Discourse on Proverbs 4:23* (Scotts Valley, CA: CreateSpace, 2016), 43.

10. John Coe, "Resisting the Temptation of Moral Formation: Moving from Moral to *Spiritual* Formation," 2005, digitalcommons.biola.edu/cgi/viewcontent.cgi?filename =0&article=1002&context=isf-lect-pre&type=additional; see also John Coe, "SFLS_02 Resisting the Temptation of Moral Formation: Moving from Moral to Spiritual Formation Pt. 2" (lecture, Biola University, La Mirada, CA, March 2006), https://digitalcommons.biola.edu/isf-lect-pre/11.

11. Ibid.

12. Priscilla Shirer, *Discerning the Voice of God: How to Recognize When God Speaks*, rev. ed. (Brentwood, TN: Lifeway Press, 2023).

13. Kyle Strobel and John Coe, "What If a Wandering Mind Is a Gift?" chap. 1 in *Where Prayer Becomes Real: How Honesty with God Transforms Your Soul* (Grand Rapids: Baker, 2021).

14. Ibid., 25.

15. Helen Howarth Lemmel, "Turn Your Eyes upon Jesus" (1922), https://hymnary.org/text/o_soul_are_you_weary_and_ troubled.

16. Elisabeth Kübler-Ross and David Kessler, *On Grief and Grieving: Finding the Meaning of Grief through the Five Stages of Loss* (New York: Scribner, 2005).

17. David Kessler, *Finding Meaning: The Sixth Stage of Grief* (New York: Scribner, 2019).

18. Ronald Rolheiser, *The Holy Longing: The Search for a Christian Spirituality*, 15th anniv. ed. (1998; repr., New York: Image, 2014), 164. References Alice Miller's famous work, *The Drama of the Gifted Child: The Search for the True Self*, rev. ed. (New York: Basic, 1997).

19. James W. Pennebaker, "Writing about Emotional Experiences as a Therapeutic Process," *Psychological Science* 8, no. 3 (May 1997): doi.org/10.1111/j.1467-9280.1997.tb00403.x; James W. Pennebaker, "Expressive Writing in Psychological Science," *Perspectives on Psychological Science* 13, no. 2 (October 2017): doi.org/10.1177/1745691617707315.

20. Tim Keller, "The Runner Christ: Our Treasury," Book of Hebrews, sermon, April 10, 2005.

21. John Calvin, *Institutes of the Christian Religion*, bk. 3, chap. 8 (1599; Bible Study Tools, accessed 2024), www.biblestudytools .com/history/calvin-institutes-christianity/book3/chapter-8 .html.

22. "New! Faith Is Spelled R-I-S-K: A Motto for Kingdom Life," Vineyard Digital, accessed January 24, 2024, vineyarddigital.org /item/new-faith-is-spelled-r-i-s-k-a-motto-for-kingdom-life/.

23. Jia Jiang, "What I Learned from 100 Days of Rejection," TED Talk at TEDxMtHood (Portland, OR: Revolution Hall at Washington High School, May 2, 2015), www.ted.com/talks /jia_jiang_what_i_learned_from_100_days_of_rejection.

24. Dietrich Bonhoeffer, *Life Together*, trans. John W. Doberstein (San Francisco: Harper, 1954), 27.

25. These four steps from Dr. John Coe were homework for me, but they've become a beautiful daily practice of befriending Jesus. Dr. John H. Coe, "Prayers of Intentions," 2013, www .redeemerlm.org/uploads/1/2/0/7/12077040/prayers_of _intention.pdf.

26. J. C. Ryle, "The Best Friend," in *Practical Religion* (1879; Project Gutenberg, 2011), www.gutenberg.org/files/38162 /38162-h/38162-h.htm#XIV.

27. I hope that's happening in heaven for Randy even though I don't think, in light of eternity being forever, that anyone is ever really old there.

28. J. I. Packer, *Knowing God* (Downers Grove, IL: InterVarsity Press, 1993), 41–42.

29. Timothy Keller, *The Meaning of Marriage: Facing the Complexities of Commitment with the Wisdom of God* (2011; repr., New York: Penguin, 2016), 44.

30. Anjuli Paschall (@lovealways.anjuli), "When I was in middle school my mom would send me to the mall with her credit card," Instagram, February 27, 2023, https://www.instagram .com/lovealways.anjuli/p/CpL5qZVpaSZ/?img_index=1.

31. Dallas Willard, *The Great Omission: Reclaiming Jesus's Essential Teachings on Discipleship* (New York: HarperOne, 2014), 61.

32. Robert Edward Luccock, *If God Be for Us: Sermons on the Gifts of the Gospel* (New York: Harper, 1954), 38.

33. This is from a Dr. Coe lecture, too. Thanks, Dr. Coe!

34. I wrote a whole different book about this, in case you're interested: Megan Fate Marshman, *Meant for Good: The Adventure of Trusting God and His Plans for You* (Grand Rapids: Zondervan, 2020).

Companion Bible Study
for Your Church or Small Group

AVAILABLE NOW

and streaming online at StudyGateway.com

Meant for Good

The Adventure of Trusting God and His Plans for You

Megan Fate Marshman

Meant for Good is a power-packed, biblical look at the truth that you really can trust God's plan for your life—no matter what your life looks like right now. Dynamic Bible teacher Megan Fate Marshman will help you discover how to stop discounting yourself from a hopeful future, start living in dependence on God, and find your way to the good plan He has for your life.

With authenticity and revelatory insights into God's character, Megan shares an engaging and fresh look at the core themes of the well-loved Scripture passage of Jeremiah 29:11-14. Through winsome and inspiring stories, *Meant for Good* will show you how to trust God in your daily life and, more important, how to trust God's definition of good above your own.

You will discover:

- That your not-enoughness is exactly enough for God, and that in fact, you have everything you need to take that first step into the life God has for you.
- How to stop counting yourself out, because Jesus never has. God is up to something really good, and He's inviting you to join Him.
- How to hear and respond to God's voice and grow a personal, intimate relationship with Him.
- How to defeat anxiety, trust God with all you're carrying and worrying about, and experience a life of freedom in relying on God daily.

God has a good plan for you—a plan to give you a hope and a future. Are you ready to believe it?

Available in stores and online!

ZONDERVAN®
.com

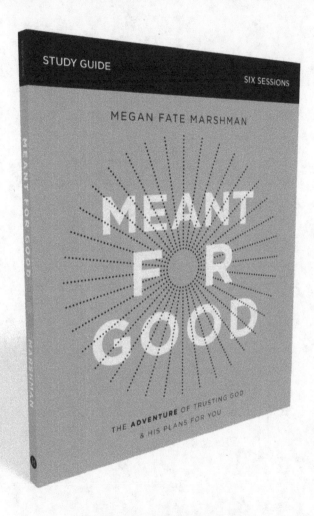
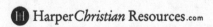

Printed in the USA
CPSIA information can be obtained
at www.ICGtesting.com
LVHW031256191124
796930LV00023B/323